D1583731

VERY UNABLE SEAMAN

1st Edition
published in 2011 by

Woodfield Publishing Ltd
Bognor Regis PO21 5EL England
www.woodfieldpublishing.co.uk

ISBN 1-84683-113-X

Printed and bound in England

Cover design by Stephanie Barr & Mike Rowland

Very Unable Seaman

*A Junior Rating's experiences
in the Royal Navy 1958-1961*

RICHARD BARR

Woodfield

Woodfield Publishing Ltd

Bognor Regis ~ West Sussex ~ England ~ PO21 5EL
tel 01243 821234 ~ e/m info@woodfieldpublishing.co.uk

Interesting and informative books on a variety of subjects

For full details of all our published titles, visit our website at
www.woodfieldpublishing.co.uk

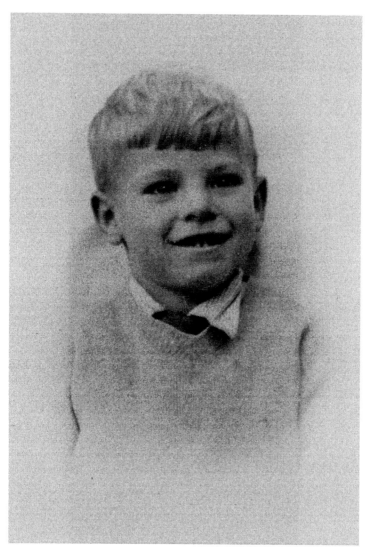

Able Seaman Barr at the age of three years.

~ CONTENTS ~

Foreword .... *iii*

Author's Preface .... *vii*

Acknowledgements .... *ix*

1. Divine Intervention 1

2. "There is also, of course, the Gunnery Branch..." 14

3. An Excursion to Scarborough 30

4. Westward Ho! 47

5. Caen, Rouen and the Unfortunate Pierre 79

6. There's Moose in My Stew Again 92

7. The Admiral Was Not Amused 116

8. A Smokescreen Over Cowes 127

9. Shooting the Balloon 148

10. What Happened Next? 160

    HMS Rampart *169*

On leave from HMS Rampart, Christmas 1960.

Foreword

Some five years after the Falklands War ended, I was invited to join the Senior NCOs of the Landing Craft and the Special Boat Service, Royal Marines, for their highly prestigious Annual Dinner; where invited guests included some of the most highly decorated and senior members of the Armed Services. To be invited was a great honour in itself but to be asked to give that year's after-dinner speech was an even greater accolade. Choosing what to say to such an august body, a collection of the most superbly qualified, experienced and – let's face it – downright dangerous warriors on the planet, was a problem. Of course, I could have taken the easy way out and told them about Fleet Clearance Diving Team Three, the group of eighteen bomb-disposal divers that I led during 'the Falklands' and who received more gallantry awards per capita than any other unit involved in the conflict – sixty six per cent. I could have told them how the Team saved two ships by removing unexploded bombs; defused and classified the first unknown, enemy sea-mine to be found since the Korean war; worked so closely with both the SBS and Landing-craft units and generally undertook many other hazardous tasks during that short period of hostilities; but I reckoned that they probably already knew that. No, what was needed was something new, yet familiar; a story to strike a chord in the hearts of serving men and grizzled veteran alike; a 'different' view of their world; and I found it in Dickie Barr's tale of HMS *Rampart* in days gone by; the history that is the subject of this book.

In today's slimmed-down, leaner, fitter and more efficient Royal Navy, it is well to remember that, not so long ago, well within living memory, the Fleet was relatively large, small ships were plentiful and 'commands' were cheap – not always going to those best suited to nor capable of assuming them. Today, every small ship the Navy has appears in Jane's Fighting Ships and their captains are as much 'in command' as the commanding officer of a frigate of destroyer. The fact that they are NCOs merely illustrates the abilities and high potential of these men. For these are the 'Little Ships' of the Royal Navy, following in the glorious line of the MTBs of the Dover Patrol, the Yangtze gunboats and the work-horses of the D-day landings.

They are as relevant now as they were then but, being fewer, are also the more valuable; yet (and was this not always the case?) un-lauded and unremembered.

> *"In worlds of violence, yet unborn,*
> *These small and frail, forgotten craft*
> *Are waiting, like their sisters*
> *Ships of Dunkerque and Zeebrugge."*

Dickie Barr is a remarkable man and has written a remarkable book. It is unassuming, without 'side' and flows so easily that it is sure to please and entertain. It is also unusual, in that it presents a view of the Navy as seen by a young man, without the constraints of latter-day 'wisdom' that so often corrupt a narrative written about events that occurred fifty years earlier. But it goes further than that. The story is told in such a way that it perfectly illustrates the unique bond held by all seafarers and Navy men in particular.

There is a closeness here that seems at odds with the rat-race to which we are all subject and the genuine regard each for the other of the Ramparts, whether Rating, Senior or Officer, becomes apparent as the tale unfolds. It is this camaraderie that is the strength of the Navy in its history, its men and its very way of thinking.

Not only will the narrative strike a chord with Veterans (as it did with those ancient Royal Marines twenty-odd years ago) but is not so technical as to exclude those unfamiliar with the workings of ships and the sea. It is, in short, a cracking good yarn – in the best traditions of seafarers and of the sea itself.

Richard and I, along with his good-wife Stephanie, have been friends since the early seventies. We have served together, adventured together, written songs and played music together and he is perhaps one of the nicest people I have ever met. He never 'looked like a PTI' (all bulging muscles and sprouting tufts of hair) yet was one of the most effective I encountered. His versatility was legendary and he rose to the zenith of his Branch. On retirement, he was honoured by HM the Queen for his services to the Royal Navy. In short, he was the right man.

Later, he was at the forefront of Britain's drive into the former Soviet Union in a bid to assist them in commercial enterprise and the 'ways of the West'.

But, in keeping with his 'small ship' upbringing, he chose to do this, not as part of some huge merchant conglomerate but, as a private enterprise and in a personal way; thus allowing similar, Eastern counterparts to establish a foothold in the free market.

So, here is RAMPART (one of the forgotten ships) in all its tawdry glory. Here you may step into the little known world of the Navy, the Dockyard and the Lower-deck – your guide, a young sailor with a priceless tale to tell. Go with him – but beware the Reindeer Stew!

Commander N A 'Bernie' Bruen MBE DSC MKhM (MCD) RN
Mazaudet, France, 2009

Passing out from HMS Raleigh, 1958. Author bottom row left.

Members of the "Then there is also, of course, the Gunnery Branch, HMS Solebay, northwest coast of Iceland, 1958. Author fourth from left.

Author's Preface

In writing this book, I have attempted to throw some light on life aboard one very small and fairly insignificant ship for one very junior able seaman of the time. It has not been my intention to create an accurate account of the history of HMS *Rampart* or that of the Royal Navy. Indeed, the events contained within this book appear very insignificant when measured against worldwide events of the period, a period during which the Royal Navy still boasted a battleship, seven aircraft carriers, several squadrons of cruisers and numerous flotillas of destroyers, frigates, submarines and small craft. Many accounts have been written by eminent historians about life in the Royal Navy and, in particular, some of the larger and more illustrious units of the fleet. Very few accounts have been written by ordinary sailors about less esteemed events, nor indeed, of life in general on the 'Lower Deck', a couple of years or so after Suez.

I am at pains to point out that events recounted herein are only as accurate as my memory of them permits, fifty years on. Indeed, as a very junior able seaman at the time, I was not privy to much first-hand information, rather, what I lived on were second- or third-hand rumours. It is true that these events have been told and retold countless times since, on other ships' mess decks and wherever else sailors gather to yarn. That they may have been embellished over the years would not be wholly unnatural. I have tried here, however, to refrain from enriching or exaggerating events and have told them as accurately as my memory permits. The broad events as they occurred are entirely true, as are all the characters. The dates and times of the events described are only as accurate as my memory and my few personal records allow.

I have changed the names of the principal characters, to prevent causing embarrassment and to protect the innocent. If what I have written embarrasses anyone, then I extend my sincerest apologies. But, shipmates, as you all used to say to me, "Barr! If you can't take it, you shouldn't have joined!"

So *déjà vu* me hearties!

Acknowledgements

I wish to convey my sincere thanks to Nick Shepperd at Woodfield Publishing Ltd. Firstly, for his kind and thoughtful words to me upon my submitting the original manuscript to him, they were a real boost to my morale at the time and, secondly, for providing me with his valuable advice and support thereafter.

I am indebted to my dear friend Bernie Bruen for agreeing to provide the foreword to this book. Also, for spending many hours correcting my English, inaccuracies in my naval vocabulary and for permitting me to use selected works of poetry of his, including 'Blake's Second Leave is Best'.

I am mindful, besides, of the numerous occasions that I have called upon my dear wife Stephanie to unravel the mess that I have created on the word processor, or to find large tracts of text that went unaccountably 'absent without leave.' Everyone in the tiny hamlet of Poyotello, high in the Sierra Segura of Andalusia, now knows how the cry, 'Stevie, I've lost all my work!' translates into Spanish.

I give thanks also to my memory, for not failing me in my hour of need.

Finally, I extend my heartfelt thanks and best wishes to all those characters, named or unnamed, within this book, who have unknowingly contributed to the writing of this account of a short but memorable period in all our lives. Without them, their comradeship, foibles, traits and personalities, there would be nothing of value to record.

R.B.
Poyotello, Spain 2011

HMS Rampart en route to Norway and the Arctic Circle, 1961.

HMS Rampart – Landing Craft Tank (LCT) L4037.

1.   Divine Intervention

From *Men of the Sea*

Are they pure kindred to the sea?
Or are they souls tormented?
Do they speak their minds out loud?
And is their case presented?

The answers they cannot be told,
The questions answered never.
They are the men who search the seas,
Their quest goes on forever.

A tribute to the RNLI by N Art Bruen

I stood at the foot of the foremast, shivering with cold and fear, clinging on for all I was worth to the lifelines secured there. In the enfolding darkness of the night, I could hear the cold, grey sea thundering by with a noise like an express train. Every few moments, tons of icy water spewed onto the main deck, completely obliterating the bridge superstructure aft of me. I felt totally alone out on the foredeck. Shielding my face from the blown spray that threatened to blind me, I squinted aloft to the cross trees, seventy feet above me, and tried to pluck up the courage to start the long, hazardous climb. Feeling for the light bulb in my oilskin pocket and at last finding the courage I needed, I started upwards. No sooner had I taken the first shaky step upon the steel-rung'd ladder than a firm hand from behind grabbed my shoulder. I turned, half expecting to see a ghost from the past. To my utter surprise, it was the Mate.

"Oh no you don't, sonny," he said. "Give me that bulb. This is no night for the likes of you to be going aloft."

He wrestled the bulb from my hand and told me to get back aft with the rest of the watch. I scurried off, glad to have been sent back to the relative safety of the deckhouse, receiving a drenching in the process. Before the watches changed and I went below, I caught up with the Mate and asked why he had not trusted me to go and replace the masthead light.

He looked at me solemnly, placed a friendly hand on my shoulder and replied, "Young Andy... twenty years ago, when I was just about your age, I was out in the Irish Sea during a storm, aboard the trawler *Kincora*. I was ordered aloft by the mate one stormy night to secure some gear that had broken loose at the masthead but at the last moment I was prevented from doing so by the Captain and owner of the ship himself, who told me to 'be off back to the deckhouse'. Before I went, however, I watched him climb until he was lost from sight in the gloom. I was the last man ever to see him alive. The next morning he was listed in the log as 'missing overboard, presumed drowned'. His name was George Simms and he was your mother's first husband. He probably saved my life that night by what he did, so I hope that goes someway to answering your question. Now be off with you."

As a child I sat, spellbound, listening to my father recount this and other stories of his early life. I have always looked upon that incident as one of divine intervention. I ask you truthfully, who could resist the call of the sea after listening to that?

My grandfather and my father's brothers had all been to sea, most of them sailing from Ringsend, Dublin, in what was then the Dublin fishing fleet. My mother and father were born in Dublin themselves. My father was just seven years of age when, during the Easter Rebellion, he was shot through the leg by a British soldier. His mother was offered, as compensation, either one hundred pounds in cash or a commission in the army for my father when he became of age. She, being almost destitute, took the money. One day during the year 1929, my father was persuaded by his cousin, Eddie Bowden, to join him as a crewman in the SS *Dunaff Head*, a ship of some 10,000 tonnes, belonging to the Ulster Steamship Company, that was sailing from the River Liffey on the evening tide. Rushing home, he told his mother what he was about to do. She remonstrated with him most passionately, having lost her first husband to the sea twenty years earlier, but to no avail; his mind was made up. He packed his belongings into a sack, bade farewell to his mother and was gone. On the way to the quay he called in briefly at BB Hopkins, Gentlemen's Outfitters, where he worked as an apprentice salesman, to give them the news. Old man Hopkins, having known his father well, tried to talk him around, but on seeing that my father's mind was made up, gave him a suit of oilskins as a farewell gift.

My father made several voyages in the ship from the china clay port of Fowey in Cornwall to Philadelphia and Montreal. Four years later, he was finally persuaded by the love of his life, later my mother, to give up the wanderlust and settle down to life ashore.

Finding work for a non-Catholic family in the Dublin of 1933 was pretty well an impossible task. When applying for work, all employers asked to know your religious leanings. When my father or mother replied 'Church of Ireland' they were invariably shown the door. Finally, realizing that their mother country no longer welcomed them as equals, they crossed the Irish Sea and found digs and jobs in Birmingham, where they worked hard and lived happily until well into their retirement. My mother and father swore their allegiance to the Monarch in the process. My father, nonetheless, never lost his wanderlust and badgered my mother enthusiastically to allow him to buy a small sailing drifter and to sail around the world with him. But she would have none of it.

"What about the children? How will they gain their schooling and how will we feed ourselves?" she would reply, following a lengthy harangue from him on the subject.

Probably through frustration, he became a commercial traveller and took himself off from Monday to Friday on journeys around the country, selling menswear and ladies wear. He often took me with him in the school holidays. Worcester, Tenbury Wells, Tewksbury, Builth Wells, Rhayader, New Radnor,

Shrewsbury and Hereford were all towns that I was fully familiar with by the age of ten. He was a great salesman, my father, but unbeknown to me at the time, there was little future in it for him. The manufacturers he travelled for could scarcely keep up with the orders he brought in, and, as he was paid commission only, he received payment just on those orders that were delivered to the customer. Expecting a bumper pay packet for the orders he had produced, he would invariably arrive home on a Friday evening and shout to my mother, "Look at this Connie! You can't keep a family on a pittance like that!" whilst banging down on the kitchen table his seven pounds-odd wages.

Following a number of other driving jobs, he settled down and became a machine setter, an occupation in which he remained until retirement. But factory life was his shackle.

I used to say to my mother, "You should have let Father buy that boat and gone around the world with him. I would have learned far more undertaking an adventure like that than I ever did at school."

"Ah, go-way, that's all very well now son," she would say, "but it was different then. I had a young family's upbringing to consider and your father was little help in the practicalities of life."

That said, we did range far and wide around England and Wales in our tiny Austin Seven.

In 1939, at Selly Oak Hospital, my mother gave birth to my brother John, a genteel and very well behaved boy. I was born two years later in 1941, in Cirencester. Heavy German bombing around Birmingham had led my mother to retreat there to the relative safety of an Aunt's house, for my birth. I was the complete opposite of my brother, being noisy and ill behaved. At the age of three, I, together with my brother, contracted whooping cough, measles and pneumonia. I remember with clarity lying in the same bed as he, kicking and shoving him in my delirium.

My mother called a doctor, who, believing me to be in a worse condition than my brother, arranged an ambulance to take me to Little Bromwich Hospital, on the far side of the city. The next day, the same doctor called to see if my brother's condition had improved. It having worsened, she left my mother, telling her that she herself would go immediately to the nearest phone box and call an ambulance for him. Over six hours later, the ambulance arrived, half an hour too late to save my brother's life. The doctor had forgotten to call the ambulance until much later in the day. My mother and father were of course devastated at the needless loss of their young son's life and, to add insult to injury, three weeks after his funeral they received a bill for the doctor's services, amounting to forty pounds, a small fortune in those days. Such was life before the NHS for ordinary folk. I recovered from these illnesses after many months convalescing, during which time my mother and father could only get across the city to visit me once each month.

When I was five, my sister Andrene arrived. Looking back to my childhood now, I feel that I treated her rather shabbily, having conspired quite innocently, on separate occasions, to cause her a broken arm, a broken leg and to be run down by the district nurse on her bicycle. This last incident occurred when she was six, whilst I was pushing her in a doll's pram and fleeing the wrath of my father for a previous misdemeanour. Looking behind to see if he was making ground on me, I did not see the district nurse on her bicycle. The next thing... crash! – and off they both gambolled down the street, sustaining no more than superficial cuts and bruises.

The broken arm was inflicted on her at the age of eight years when my school friends and I put her to good use as a temporary goalpost. She stopped a wet and soggy football with her arm instead of dodging it, as most sensible girls of eight might have done. The broken leg occurred three years later, in a public park and on being encouraged by me to come down a slide that had had the bottom two sections removed. That she ever forgave me is to her lasting credit.

Our summer school holidays were usually taken at 26 Pearce Street in Dublin, in rooms belonging to my grandparents. These were situated on two floors above BB Hopkins, Gentlemen's

Outfitters, very close to the city centre and where my father had worked prior to going off to sea.

During the war years, my grandparents could not buy tea or sugar, these items being even more severely rationed in Ireland than in England. My mother saved part of her tea ration each week for a year and then, just prior to departing for Dublin, stuffed the whole lot into a home-made teddy-bear and sealed the seams. I carried the teddy through customs unknowingly on many occasions. I gave my parents a dreadful fright one night when passing through customs at Holyhead. I was mindlessly swinging the teddy-bear round and round by one leg, hitting it on the table, upon which our bags were being examined by a customs officer. My mother thought that, at any moment, the stitching would give way and that tea would fly everywhere. She had visions of being led off into custody. Fortunately for all of us, her stitching was up to the highest standard and our petty smuggling went unobserved.

There was no garden or yard at 26 Pearce Street and my parents, try as they might, could not keep me indoors. From the age of ten, I would nag my mother and father unremittingly to allow me outside. Such was my persistence that they had little option but to relent. Once out, I roamed the centre of Dublin, becoming intimate with its busy streets, places of interest and the vocabulary of its inhabitants. With three pence in my pocket, I would visit the Cafola in Westmorland Street or the Kardoma in O'Connell Street and sit there, boggle-eyed behind the most enormous knickerbocker-glory available. I even wandered over to the other side of the city to the great Phoenix Park. My greatest pleasure, however, was upon leaving Pearce Street, to turn left down into Shaw Street and onto the south quay wall of the river Liffey, just below the Butt Bridge, in those days the last bridge crossing the Liffey before the docks and the open sea. I wandered along the quayside for hours on end, watching cargo being loaded into the holds of ships of a dozen or more nations, dodging between horse-drawn drays, motor lorries and swinging crane jibs. I watched enthralled as ships of all shapes and sizes arrived and departed. I was in my element on the occasions that one of the Guinness Company ships, *The Lady Grannia*, was alongside, because my uncle Eddie, the cousin who had persuaded my father to go to sea with him years before, was her master. I would clamber aboard amid the clatter of thousands of barrels of Guinness being loaded and seek him out.

"Ah young Richard, and where do you want to sail off to today?" he would say, before taking me up to the bridge and sticking me behind the binnacle. Then he would commence giving me wheel orders. I would spin the wheel and repeat the orders back to him.

On the occasions when his ship was at sea, I would walk down instead to where the River Dodder joined the Liffey, cross the Iron Bridge near Ringsend and walk right out as far as the Pool Beg Light, hoping to see her return. The lighthouse was as far out as you could go before dropping into the Irish Sea. On one side of me was the entrance to the Liffey and beyond it Hoath Head. On the other side was Sandymount Bay. I could look right across to Sandymount, Booterstown and Dún Laoghaire. What blissful days they were. And what risks I ran, had I but known it.

For one thing, I could not swim an inch and I spent many hours gazing down sheer quay walls into the oily water of the Liffey. My parents and grandparents would be beside themselves with worry, as I would often be gone for the whole of the day and sometimes well into the evening. When I returned, first my father would haul me up onto the landing and rap my knuckles, then in turn grandfather, grandmother and any aunts or uncles who happened to be in the house at the time, and there were often many, would have their say. I felt the full force of their tongues and the backs of their hands on many occasions.

Days later, an aunt or uncle would call in and say to me, "So you're the little brat that's giving your mammy and daddy all the grief, are you not now?" and when I proffered a response would continue, "Don't you know that little boys should be seen and not heard?"

I would not be deterred, however, and in a few days I would find myself once again out in the city or on its busy quays. I was always a restless spirit and was eventually taken by my mother to visit specialists at the Children's Hospital in Birmingham. I hated going there and ran away at the last moment whenever I could. Having to leave school during class time singled me out unfairly as an oddball. The teacher would look at the clock and shout out, "Richard Barr! Your mother is waiting outside in the hall for you." All the other kids would snigger as I left the classroom.

On one occasion, I ran away just as the bus drew up. When, hours later, we arrived late for my appointment, the specialist told my mother that she was more in need of help than I was. It was as a direct result of these visits that I was eventually diagnosed as suffering from Chorea or St Vitus' Dance, as it is more commonly known.

"Keep him indoors and keep him quiet, no excitement whatsoever," was the remedy offered.

Fat chance my parents had of maintaining that regime! I even escaped from my first floor bedroom window one lovely summer's evening, by dropping to the garden below, when all of my friends were out playing cricket in the street. I was just twelve years old when, one day several weeks later, I was kept away from school for the day. Thinking it was another trip to the specialist, I was contemplating just how to escape it but before I could formulate a plan, two elderly ladies in a car called at our house in Kings Heath.

After chatting to my mother for a while, they pointed in my direction. Shortly afterwards I was taken firmly by the hand and bundled, with a packed suitcase, into an old black Hillman Minx. We drove for several hours, eventually arriving at a small cottage in the middle of nowhere, on a hill called The Hope, seven miles north of Ludlow in Shropshire. Here I was to stay for a year and a half with a farmer and his wife, Jack and Lucy

Martin. I was heartbroken on arrival but they turned out to be two of the strictest yet fairest people I ever knew. They were also extremely philanthropic, for they often had 'difficult boys like me' to stay with them.

After the first agonising month, I got over my homesickness and gradually came to love it there. Outdoor life was definitely for me and I had plenty of it. The cottage, contained within its own large apple orchard, had no electricity or water and its only source of heating was from the kitchen range. There was another lad my age staying with them, Bill Wheldon, also from Birmingham. On occasion there were even three of us at a time staying there.

My daily task, before leaving to catch the school bus in the morning, was to fetch several pails of water from a tap at the bottom of the apple orchard and fill the water butt. One of my weekly tasks was to empty the dry toilet and bury its contents in a field at the back. Woe betide you if you forgot where you had buried the previous week's offering; you would very soon know about it when you started digging the new hole.

In the evenings, during the winter months, playing cards was our only form of entertainment. I learned to play Whist, Rummy, Chase the Lady and Nominations, all under the glow of a paraffin lamp. In the summer months, I roamed far and wide – to Stanton Lacy, Stokesay and Haytons Bent. It was there I first smoked a cigarette and drove a car. I say 'drove' a car. What I mean is, on the way home from church one Sunday morning I came upon an old Austin Seven that was parked in a rutted lane. Being ultra-inquisitive, I went around to the front and, seeing the starting handle, gave it a quick swing like my father used to do. To my utter surprise and horror, it sprang to life and leapt forward, giving me the ride of my life on top of the radiator for twenty or thirty yards, until it hit a low embankment, thus projecting me over the top of it. The car had been left in gear and was apparently the sort not in need of an ignition key.

Scared to death, I left it there and ran home, saying nothing to anyone about it. The following day, Lucy let drop the hint that the police were out looking for a suspected car thief. I owned up immediately and was told to go and apologise the next day to the owner of the car, a neighbouring farmer. Jack came with me and upon meeting the farmer there was much shaking of heads and "you be a-goin' to hurt yourself one of these fine days, young scallywag..." and suchlike.

Jack and he spoke for a short while in muffled tones, after which I was instructed by the farmer to harvest all of the apples from his orchard that autumn, to teach me a lesson. I suppose it was a bit like community service. It was a task that took me three weeks of evenings until bedtime and weekends.

Before I left Jack and Lucy to return to my parents, I had also contrived to have myself expelled from the secondary school I attended in Ludlow. One day, a boy's dinner money went missing and the local children and their families, all being well known to the school, were considered above such a felony. I, on the other hand, was from the big city, and not so well known at all. There could be only one outcome. Although I pleaded innocent to all charges, I was not believed.

"Own-up and you may be forgiven," said the Headmaster.

"I didn't take it," I maintained, knowing full well that I was blameless. Jack and Lucy fought my corner but to no avail.

"You will never come to any good young lad," the Headmaster told me finally, and so, to a degree, I grew up believing that I wouldn't. I was then summarily dismissed from the school with the headmaster's words, "You city folk come here to the country and bring your bad habits with you," ringing in my ears.

I was just short of my fourteenth birthday when I returned home to my parents under a cloud and re-started school in a large and impersonal suburban secondary school. With my heart no longer in it, I was allowed to spend much of my lesson time in the school greenhouse, potting geranium cuttings and sowing seeds. I left school four months short of my fifteenth birthday, found digs near Redditch and started my working life...

I first went to work as a young farm hand on a farm in Worcestershire, where the gentleman farmer I worked for, an ex-colonel, insisted upon bellowing to me at the top of his voice, "BOY!" The work was hard and the hours long and I was expected to do a man's work for a boy's pay of eleven shillings a week. One day, two Hungarian refugees, fleeing from the Russian invasion, came and joined the workforce of twelve. For some light relief, we had great fun playing them at football in the old yard at dinnertime. The pair of them were so skilful that we could not even get the ball off them. Several months later, they went to start a new life in Canada.

Failing to settle to farm working, I tried my hand at engineering, going to work in a factory as a trainee machine setter. I fared no better there, so my father one day suggested to me that I should give serious consideration to going to sea. For several weeks he worked at persuading me, showing me glowing newspaper advertisements expounding the virtues of joining the Royal Navy and seeing the world. I was then sixteen and a half and had been in work for nearly two years. He therefore further emphasised that I would not have to join as a boy seaman, which was what the advertisement indicated. *Ah! A little recognition from Father of something achieved ... unusual that!* I thought at the time, forgetting that I had achieved so little worthy of praise up to then anyway.

Eventually, just prior to Christmas 1957, I finally gave in to the pressure. There were two reasons for my change of heart. The first, and by far the most serious at that moment in time, was that I had just been dismissed from my latest job as a trainee toolmaker. After leaving the farm, an uncle of mine had, through a contact of his, procured for me a job at Kings Heath Engineering Ltd, telling me that one day, if I studied hard and knuckled down to it, I could become a toolmaker like him. In the event, I was dismissed after barely five months for 'lack of attention to detail'. I had – not surprisingly for me at the time – overlooked the necessity to anchor down a sizable chunk of metal casting to the table of a side-and-face-grinder, which I had been given licence for the first time to practice on unsupervised. Inevitably, truly spectacular results were achieved when what was left of the casting after the rapidly spinning cutter made contact with it was propelled at the speed of sound across the workshop floor, ricocheting off a temporarily unmanned milling machine before demolishing the foreman's work desk.

I stood rooted to the spot, terrified, whilst everyone else within range dived for cover amid the cacophony of colliding metal, shouts of anguish and splintering wood. Luckily for me, no one was hurt, although someone could easily have been killed.

"I didn't' do it!" I protested, without much conviction or to anyone in particular, as heads and bodies finally emerged from behind protective machinery or stanchions. To the workshop foreman, when I had fully recovered my senses, I said, "I did everything that I was shown, honestly I did."

"You could have maimed someone you stupid little sod! Have you got nothing more to say for yourself?' And, after a pregnant silence, 'No? Then come with me...'"

With that, he marched me stiffly along the shop floor to the workshop manager's office, where I was told to wait outside. All those around me on the shop floor were shaking their heads, giving me knowing glances; one or two younger ones like myself gave me the 'cut throat' sign. After what seemed an eternity, I was beckoned to enter. I stood nervously in front of the works manager as he told me, in extremely adult terms, that my future did not lie in engineering and that, under no circumstances, would it lie in this factory. The adult terms used to inform me of this left me a little confused for some weeks. There being inferences to body parts I had never heard of up to then. They were invectives that I felt I could not repeat to my mother or father. Before I left, however, I was told that, as I had paid into the firm's Christmas Party fund, I would be permitted to attend. I did so and got drunk for the first time in my life.

The second reason for taking my father's advice was, looking back on it, somewhat more disturbing than the first. Two streets away from where I lived in Kings Heath was a corner shop,

Grice's Greengrocer and Fruiterer. I had to pass the shop on my way to and from the factory where I worked. The Grices' daughter, Paula, was a very slim, well-developed and outgoing sort of girl, about a year younger than me, who had got into the habit of waylaying me on my way home from work.

Having entrapped me on more than one occasion as I passed by, "for a chat about things, music and the like," she would say, Paula began making advances that I just did not know how to handle. Don't misunderstand, I wanted to touch, as it were, but I just didn't have the bottle. My brain always froze over when in her company, completely and utterly anaesthetised. I would stand there in front of her with a sick grin, stupefied, not knowing what to do or say. Frankly, I was terrified of her and would go to any lengths to avoid her, including making great detours each day.

My mother, who liked the Grices very much, invited her to my sixteenth birthday party. Yes, some mothers still did that in the fifties. The result was that when I found what she had done, I bunked off to the cinema alone to see 'The Cockleshell Heroes', thus offending both my dear mother and the Grices' daughter into the bargain.

I thought joining the Navy would at least put some distance between Paula and me. And so it did.

Years later, when casting my mind back, I thought what pleasures might have accrued had I been less self-conscious at the time but such were the circumstances under which I duly completed and posted to Royal Navy Recruiting, an application form, signed by myself, my father and our local vicar. The latter, presumably, to attest that I was a fine upstanding youth who could be trusted not to be taken advantage of by fifteen-year-old greengrocers' daughters.

Just what the Navy were looking for!

A couple of weeks later, having first received an invitation by post, I presented myself, as directed, to the Royal Navy recruiting office in James Watt Street, Birmingham to await my fate.

2. "There is also, of course, the Gunnery Branch..."

From *Mighty Tall Ships*

Mighty tall ships and graceful clippers
That once sailed proudly on the breeze,
Their days were numbered like leaves of summer
And now they have vanished from the seas.
The seas they raged and the wind it roared,
As they sailed down to Rio and Cape Horn,
"All hands up aloft lads, take in the canvas,
And we'll ride this gale out 'til dawn."

    Richard Barr

Arriving outside the recruiting office, I walked to and fro in front of it several times, trying to look through the window without being observed from within. Finally, having been able to see very little, I entered. A very smart naval rating invited me to sit with a group of other youths approximately my own age. I did as directed and slowly took in my surroundings. I noticed that behind the desk over to my left was a rotund Chief Petty Officer. He sported a weather-beaten face and a disarming smile that suggested it had been carried around the world and into a few bars in its time. He was talking in animated tones to a young lad like me, who was sitting in front of him.

On the wall behind him, hung two, large wall posters. One of them was a photograph of a group of smiling ratings in white tropical uniform being guided around some Greek temple or other, whilst the other showed what looked like the self-same ratings, enjoying a day out on the water in a rowing-boat. To the right of him, in a glass case, was a huge model of a battleship with a large White Ensign on the wall behind. At another desk to the right of me was a Sergeant of the Royal Marines, sat as upright as a fireman's pole and speaking to another lad in front of him in clear clipped tones.

"Becoming a Royal Marine is a calling not a fancy, my young man. It requires lots of hard work, courage and endeavour," I heard him say, looking the youngster straight in the eye.

I had never seen a Royal Marine in real life before and immediately thought of 'The Cockleshell Heroes', danger and adventure.

'Hmmm!' I thought. 'That could do me.' Then, directly behind him, my eyes fell upon a large black and white picture that portrayed Royal Marine Commandos, with blacked faces and packs the size of houses strapped to their backs, spewing out of boats and up a beach somewhere, looking very determined, very wet and very cold. Another photograph showed a group of them, one behind the other, bending to one side with a telegraph pole on their shoulders, doing PT presumably.

Turning to the fellow sitting next to me, I ventured out of the corner of my mouth, "They must me joking, expecting anyone to join the Marines."

He looked at me obliquely and said very curtly, "Well I am," and turned back to the brochure he had been reading.

I was about to probe him further on the subject when the chair in front of the sergeant was vacated and he was beckoned across to fill it. He was a big, strapping lad, well over six feet, and seemed brim full of self-confidence. I looked down at my skinny five feet eight in my pumps, glanced at the poster behind the sergeant, then across at the friendly face of the Chief, and instantly made up my mind. It was the Navy for me.

I sat a good half an hour before my turn came. When it did, 'Chiefy' welcomed me with unnerving bonhomie. He positively exuded friendliness. Shaking my hand, he said, "Well son, if you are set upon joining the Navy, then we will have to see what we can do to help you."

I looked behind me, thinking for one moment that he was addressing someone else before I realized that he was talking to me. No one had ever said anything like that to me before.

"Err, well not exactly..." I said, haltingly, feeling that things were moving too fast. "It's my father, actually, he suggested that I ... err ... come and talk to you."

"And jolly sensible he is too," he replied. "Sit down here." He offered me the chair in front of his desk.

I was then asked all sorts of questions, some fairly straightforward, like 'Do you have two functioning arms and legs?' and 'What is the colour of that flag over there?' pointing to a red pennant in one corner. Then others, rather more obscure, like, 'Do you enjoy the company of girls?' and 'Did you attend an all boys' school?'

I shrank from telling him the saga of my brushes with the greengrocer's daughter. I didn't want him to jump to the wrong conclusions, so I mumbled something like, "I am more interested in my future than girls at the moment" and "all my schools were mixed."

"Right you are then," he replied, his lines of enquiry seemingly satisfied. Finally, he got round to asking "What branch of the service would you most like to join?"

Now I felt we were getting somewhere.

"I've not given it much thought but I certainly don't want to be either a steward or a stoker. Maybe a signalman," I said, probably too enthusiastically, remembering scenes from *The Cruel Sea* where a signalman on the ship's bridge was sending off, by lamplight, his message, rat-a-tat-tat-a-tat. The thought of spending the rest of my life in the bowels of a ship's boiler room or stokehold was too hideous to contemplate, while becoming a steward did not really have the aura of *sailorizing* that I was quickly becoming interested in.

"I see from your application form that you are a trainee machine setter. Perhaps you would like to give some consideration to entering as an Artificer," he proffered.

With the severe bollocking I had received at the hands of the machine workshop manager still resounding in my ears, and feeling ashamed to tell him that I had been sacked, I plucked up courage from somewhere and said, "No, I will settle for becoming a signalman, if you don't mind."

With that, he drew back, sucked at the end of his pen, frowned, then sighed and ultimately consulted the sheaf of papers in front of him. Eventually he looked up at me and said most earnestly, "Well, there may be a long wait as we seem to be oversubscribed for entry into that branch at present. Now, however, if you were to consider joining the seaman branch, well, we could have you in and training in a matter of weeks and there are so many more options open to you. There are three sub-branches for you to choose from; Radar plotting for example, Torpedo and Anti-Submarine or even Gunnery..."

The seductive way in which he went on to portray life as a seaman had me hanging on to his every word. Like a good angler, Chiefy knew when he had got his fish well and truly hooked and was not about to let this one slip off the end of his line. The résumé finally complete, he said with authority, "Of course you understand that only the most accomplished are selected to become radar plotters. But you must also not lose sight of the fact that entry into the Torpedo and Anti-Submarine Branch requires men who have alert minds and are quick thinking." Then, almost as an afterthought, he added, "Then there is also, of course, the Gunnery Branch..."

Many years later, when my ears were ringing and my eyes were streaming from cordite smoke, I pondered over this last, almost nonchalant remark and felt that I should have pressed him further on what he meant by it, but before I knew it, he had pushed a paper in my direction and invited me to sign it. "There and there," he pointed, whilst at the same time telling me that the sub-branch I was selected for, would be decided as I went through initial training and so "not to worry about a thing." After I had signed where shown, he jumped up, shook me by the hand, gave me some nice coloured brochures to show my parents and, opening the door for me, said, "You will be hearing from us soon with further instructions. Goodbye and Good Luck!"

I walked away down the street to catch my bus home with a . greater sense of purpose that I had ever had before. When I arrived home the first thing my father said was, "Well... have you done it?"

On February 4th 1958, just 2 months after being informed that, "Then there is also, of course, the Gunnery Branch..." I caught a train from New Street Station, bound for Plymouth, with instructions to join HMS *Raleigh*, the new entry training establishment at Torpoint, for initial training. I was just three months short of my seventeenth birthday. Little did I imagine then, as I passed for the first time through the main gate of HMS *Raleigh* as a civilian about to become a sailor, that twenty eight and a half years later I would pass through it in the opposite direction for the last time, as a Warrant Officer about to become a civilian again.

Six months training followed in a blur. Almost the entire intake that week was recruited from the Glasgow area, so my classmates, with few exceptions, spoke with a brogue I found hard to comprehend. Being a 'Brummie' myself, I and one or two others from different parts of England were singled out for special treatment by the 'Jocks' from the first day. I soon learned that I had to fight my corner or go under – but with twenty of them to contend with, it was hard work.

The only noteworthy occurrence was my learning to swim. One day, all of my class was mustered on the poolside and divided off into those that could and those that couldn't swim. We, the could-nots, were called 'backward swimmers' and were, to my horror, herded down to the deep end of the pool.

"Here," I said to the chappie next to me, "there is something wrong with this arrangement. All the swimmers are up at the shallow end while we, the non-swimmers, are at the deep end."

Then, four at a time, we were told to jump out into the water with instructions to swim as best we were able to the other end.

I had never been in a swimming pool before in my life and hadn't the remotest idea how to stay afloat, let alone start to swim. When my turn came, I remember being overcome with dread. I had watched several others flounder before me, only to be fished out with long poles held by the instructors. Closing my eyes tightly, I flung myself out, trying to catch hold of the rail along the side of the pool, but my grasping hands were beaten off by one of the long poles. Flailing my arms like a paddleboat, my eyes screwed tightly shut, I clawed my way around the pool more under the water that above the surface, until eventually, I managed to touch the bottom. I had propelled myself twelve yards up the pool and was delirious with joy, principally, I think, because I was still alive. Later, I went on to become one of the pole holders and to teach numerous others to swim, but all that was still in the distant future.

In the event, I was considered insufficiently 'accomplished' for training as a radar plotter. Neither was I alert nor quick thinking enough to become an effective torpedo man and so, by complete accident, I fell into 'then there is also, of course, the Gunnery Branch...' Now, even within this, the largest of the three seamen sub-branches, would you believe, there were three further sub-categories? The ablest of those remaining were selected to train to become *gun controllers*, ratings who manned the nice warm transmitting stations deep within the ship and the less cosy control directors high up in the foretops. The slightly less able, though perhaps more astute than me, were selected to train to become *gun layers* and *gun trainers*, who manned the noisy gun turrets laying and training them onto their targets. Finally, there were those of us 'also-rans' who tried hard but were just not able or astute enough. We became *gunnery quarters ratings* and were trained to man the gun bays, shell rooms and magazines.

Upon finishing training and seeing the results of my gunnery course posted on the training department notice board, I turned away deflated and said silently to myself, 'Well, if you start from the very bottom, there is really only one way you can go, and that is upwards.' But wait a minute. What was I thinking? I was not a steward and neither was I a stoker. I had therefore, in my mind at least, achieved something. So life wasn't so bad after all.

On completion of training in October 1958, I was drafted to Royal Naval Barracks Portsmouth to await my first ship. In November that year I joined HMS *Solebay*, a Battle Class Destroyer and leader of the First Destroyer Squadron. In her, I served a commission as an Ordinary Seaman.

I played my tiny part in the Cod War, patrolling off the north east coast of Iceland for six weeks over Christmas 1958, deterring the Icelandic gunboat *Thor* from molesting our fishermen. Then, designated East of Suez, the ship sailed, in April 1959, for the Far East for a year. During that time we visited, amongst other places of interest, Dubai (when it was still just a small fishing port without even a quay), Bahrain and Karachi (where I was invited into the household of a Pakistani family and tasted my first ever curry). There followed Trincomolee in Ceylon (now Sri Lanka), Singapore, Hong Kong and, in Australia, Albany, Townsville, Mackay, Brisbane and Melbourne (for Christmas 1959). I was also privileged to visit some of the world's most historic sights: the *Scuizo Bar* in Gibraltar, the *Malta Gut* in Valletta, *The Street of a Thousand Arseholes* in Istanbul, *Bhugis Street* in Singapore and the *Wanchai Sampans* in Hong Kong. What an apprenticeship!

During that year away, we exercised with many other navies of the Commonwealth and responded to an SOS from a merchant ship in the South China Sea, then salvaged it and towed it to Manila in the Philippines. I received two pounds and fourteen shillings as my share of the salvage, having, with a few others, done what we thought then was most of the hard work. Over on the lifeless freighter we had hauled in by hand what seemed like miles of six-inch manila towing hawser and much of the anchor cable.

We also spent considerable time blockading the Sunda Straits between Java and Sumatra against passage of Soviet oil tankers supplying Indonesian insurgents. On return to Portsmouth, in May 1960, the ship paid off and I was drafted once again to the Royal Naval Barracks to await my next ship.

So now here I was, in October 1960, loaned from barracks, to the aircraft carrier HMS *Albion*, in Portsmouth Dockyard, to help paint the ship. I travelled daily between barracks and Albion. In barracks, I lived in one of several large, two storey Victorian accommodation blocks, called mess decks. Each block housed around four hundred men on two floors. The mess decks were large, open plan and extremely draughty. Beds were arranged two high, in four rows of fifty, lengthwise on each mess deck. In a cleared space in the centre of each mess deck was a large coke-burning stove. Arranged around it were up to sixty red vinyl easy chairs. The bathroom and toilets for each floor were outside. The coke stove was the only source of heating. At pipe down (lights out) the stove was emptied and the cinders were taken outside to a specially constructed *cinder bin*. The stove could be relit the next day at noon.

It was one of those typically cold, blustery days in late autumn with grey, rain-sodden clouds scudding down the harbour on a chilling sea breeze. It served to remind me that the onset of winter was just around the corner. We matelots were clinging like spiders to a giant web of a scrambling net suspended from Albion's flight deck.

It was 'paint ship' time and the twenty or so of us from Royal Naval Barracks had been lent to the ship for five weeks to assist the permanent crew to give her a new coat of paint, a giant undertaking. *Albion* was due to sail for the Far East before Christmas and the rush was on to complete her in time. We had been loaned because we were all 'between ships' ourselves.

The rope and wire net we were working from was bowsed in underneath the vast overhang of the flight deck on the port side, which made it fairly easy for us, the occupants, to get into reasonably comfortable painting positions, standing or leaning back in the net whilst working. From where I was perched I had an unobstructed view across the harbour-reaches towards

Portchester and its castle. In the middle distance I could make out row upon row of mothballed ships of the Reserve Fleet clustered together like old men seeking companionship and warmth in their retirement. They looked crestfallen, forsaken and unwanted. Amongst them, there were several cruisers and destroyers and an array of frigates, sloops, minelayers, minesweepers and other small craft. In their midst, there stood out boldly the cruisers *Gambia* and *Kenya* and the aircraft carriers *Theseus* and *Leviathan*.

What stories could they all tell? I mused. Not so long ago they had been humming, vibrant ships of the fleet but a ship without a crew, its company and family, is just another shapely hulk of steel or wood without a soul. Those ships that individually and collectively had achieved such glory for their country now waited, uncomplainingly, their turn for the final calling, the inevitable trip to the breakers yard and oblivion. Only in the memories of the men who served in them, would they ultimately be remembered. It was a truly melancholy sight.

In the harbour closer by, a water taxi growled its way past, heading towards Whale Island, its cargo of passengers huddled together in the lee of a flimsy superstructure, trying to escape the clutches of an autumn wind. A large and powerful paddle tug passed it close by, heading in the opposite direction, its bluff bow breasting the chop, sending spray high into the air. I watched as the water taxi bit into its bow wave, throwing salt spray across its passengers and heard their curses way up there in my scrambling net. Over on the Gosport side of the harbour, I could make out a cluster of pulling whalers heading in behind the old French triple-decker *Fourdroyant* and away towards the shore. Their crews looked for the entire world like young seamen from HMS *St Vincent*, the boys training establishment. They leaned back on their oars, straining to make headway against the wind and tide, the voices of their coxswains, calling out the stroke, drifting plaintively across the water.

From this side of the ship, I could not see the dockside but I could hear its familiar sounds: the frightful rattle of windy hammers chipping old paint and rust from steel plating, the deep rumble of motor transport wending its way amongst the jetties and thumping loudly as it crossed the caissons of the dry docks, the continuous hum of machinery from countless workshops, the hissing of steam escaping from pressurised boilers, the occasional 'toot-toot' of the dockside railway and the strident sounds of ships' quartermasters making announcements over their Tannoy systems. There were aromas too: of burning steel, new paint, tar, rope, diesel and steam, the reassuring sounds and smells of the world within which I now lived.

Between taking in the scenery and indulging in the familiarity of my surroundings, I was mindlessly dabbing grey topcoat paint to row upon row of protruding rivet heads that secured Albion's massive plates to her stout frames, making it easier for those following on behind with long handled rollers, to complete the job speedily. It was cold, tedious, monotonous work that called for a minimum of concentration on the painting front, yet maximum ability to hang for dear life to your pot and brush. To lose either of those was tantamount to mutiny in the eyes of 'Jimmy the One' [the first lieutenant]. It would most certainly provoke his wrath and in addition, have the cost of replacing them deducted from your pay. To bring upon your shoulders the wrath of the first lieutenant, in any ship, was to be avoided at all costs, especially for an Able Seaman who valued his liberty, while to fall out of the net and into the harbour yourself might bring perhaps only the mildest of rebukes from the Jimmy but was certain to bring you lots of badinage such as 'you silly wanker' from your shipmates. I was keen to avoid either.

I was roused suddenly out of my daydreaming by a raucous bellowing from the ship's pinnace[1] forty yards or so off the port bow, "Barr! If you don't shove that fucking brush into top gear sometime soon I will have you back here on your own in the dog

---

[1] A pinnace is a general purpose motor boat.

watches and at the weekend besides, savvy?" I knew intuitively that it was the voice of the Petty Officer of the Side Party, to whom I had been allocated for work whilst in the ship.

I had been so absorbed in my thoughts that when his voice carried up to me from below and exploded in my ears, I not unnaturally jumped to oblige, something a young able seaman did quite instinctively when bellowed at by a Petty Officer. But in the act of obliging, I lost my balance and my hold on the netting, toppled sideways and groped with both hands for support. Then I watched, horrified, as though in slow motion, first my pot and then my brush descended the best part of thirty feet into the water below, landing with a loud 'splaaduunk! I lay in the net for a moment, spread-eagled, hanging on for dear life to prevent myself from following my pot and brush downwards and making up a threesome. I badly wanted to be reunited with them but not that badly. Lying there, looking down, I marvelled at the rapidly expanding circle of ripples, streaked with grey marbling effect, spreading outwards on the surface from the point of entry of my pot and brush. It looked like a beautiful mosaic. A few moments elapsed before the inevitable bellicose expletives rose up to me from the pinnace – "How could any mother give birth to such a dickhead as you?" etc – whilst other, rather more supportive comments drifted down from my fellow incumbents in the net. I remember thinking to myself, 'Why didn't the Chiefy in Birmingham's recruiting office acquaint me with this peril when he was expounding the joys of becoming a seaman?' Just then, to add insult to injury, I felt wet paint dripping on my head from above. Looking upwards, I located its source. It was from the pot of the 'tosser' clinging on directly above me, whose equilibrium had been disturbed by my clumsiness. The realization slowly dawned upon me that I would probably have to forfeit part of my meagre able seaman's pay for the loss of the pot and brush. Besides which, as if that were not punishment enough, I may have my liberty curtailed. I didn't feel like a jolly sailor just then. It had all been going so well recently and now my weekend leave could be in jeopardy.

In those days, sailors had, by and large, fairly simple needs. Among the most prized of these were beer, women and liberty. To me, liberty was the foremost. The prospect of having my much longed-for long- weekend leave pass cancelled was very painful indeed. At that moment, the gods held out just the teeniest offering of relief from the haranguing I was still receiving from the pinnace below, the Petty Officer therein seemingly unable to come to grips with the idea that I actually had parents who were married before I was born. The relief came in the guise of the voice of the quartermaster over the ship's Tannoy, announcing the 'stand easy' (tea break). It served to bring me back to sanity. I climbed gingerly down through the netting and inboard onto the foc's'le to the inevitable chorus of "You wanker!" from my shipmates. Ignoring them, I cleaned the paint from my head and shoulders as best I could with cotton waste and white spirits before wending my way down to the 'on-loan seamen's mess deck' for my tea, over a hot steaming mug of which, I fended off, as best I could, the mocking remarks of those I had been working with in the netting that morning.

I was startled out of my ambivalence upon hearing my name announced over the ship's Tannoy. *'Able Seaman Barr, report to the Regulating Office* (ship's police station).*'*

There was always something unnerving about hearing one's name called out on a ship's Tannoy, particularly in connexion with 'the Regulating Office'. It implied, 'We know something about you and want to talk with you about it but you cannot get an instant answer. You're in limbo until you get to see the person or persons responsible for sending the message. It took me a long time to overcome this feeling. I used to automatically think, 'Shit! I must be in the rattle (trouble) again'. This time was no exception.

'Here we go,' I thought, suspecting that my next long- weekend leave was about to be cancelled over the pot and brush incident. I swallowed the last dregs of tea, washed out my mug in the *fanny* (like a large dixie) provided, stuck two fingers up at the crowded mess offering me friendly advice on what I should bloody well tell them, and hurried up to the Regulating Office two decks up, mentally preparing myself for the worst.

"Able Seaman Barr here, Chief," I reported when I entered.

"Ah! There you are. I've got a draft chit here for you. Whose boots have you been licking then?" This was disobligingly uttered by what I took to be the duty regulating petty officer, who had his face stuck in an oversized tin mug at the time.

"Pardon?" I said, unable to take in the magnitude of the statement. "I've got a draft chit, arrived here for you from barracks," he repeated, lowering the mug to his desktop.

Now, when you are so abruptly presented with information of that enormity, it is capable of creating all manner of turmoil within, such as trepidation, excitement or just plain resignation. What it meant in reality was *change* – change of shipmates, change of ship, change of job, possibly change of home port, of everything that you may have become accustomed to – and, given that the Royal Navy of the fifties still ranged far and wide across the world, it could mean *really big change*. Normally, you could expect some sort of advance notice or even a smidgen of choice regarding where you were to be drafted next. Notwithstanding, I recovered my composure and inwardly became excited. The prospect of becoming a part of a proper ship's company once again was far preferable to being, as I was presently, loaned out here for a week, there for another couple of weeks and so on, as part of a labour gang. I must have been in a half–trance.

"Are you with me *Sonny*? I said I have a draft chit here for you to join HMS *Rampart* immediately," he repeated rather testily, placing greater emphasis on the word 'sonny' than I felt was warranted at the time.

"Err... what's that? Where is it? Where's it going PO?" I stammered. These are key things a sailor needs to know when he gets a draft chit and all I could think of saying, seeing as how this was the very last piece of news I was expecting to hear. I was all booked up to go up the line to see my 'party' (girlfriend) at the weekend. That could now be in jeopardy for the second time today. *This is a bombshell to beat all bombshells*, I thought to myself.

"The answer to your first, second and third questions, sonny," he replied, "is *I don't know*." But he did have the good grace eventually to disclose that he thought *Rampart* may be somewhere here in the dockyard. "Now you had better go and get this leaving routine completed, return your loan clothing and report back to barracks, your parent ship. They will have all the answers to your questions."

The routine of joining and leaving a ship in the Navy is a ritual. On leaving, it serves to ensure that your account is cleared up, all items borrowed are returned or, if lost, paid for and your records and documents are completed to follow you later to your new ship. Joining your new ship opens your account, enables you to draw items of temporary gear and introduces your arrival to those who most need to know, such as the Pay Office, the Victualling Office, your Divisional Officer, etc. I took the card and turned away, hoping to get back to the mess to tell my mates about my good fortune but by the time I arrived there, they had all turned to again, so I lost out on 'having the last word.' I managed to avoid the PO of the Side Party for the rest of the morning while I ran around getting stamps and signatures on the back of my leaving card. As I was on loan, there were not many of these required. I changed out of overalls into No 8s (working rig), packed my few belongings and was off over the gangway.

At this rate I should get to barracks in time for dinner, I thought.

Back in barracks, I completed the larger part of my leaving routine that afternoon, omitting only the bedding store until morning. At the Pay Office, the PO Writer handed me a sub (a small advance of pay) as this was a pay week and I would not be in barracks to draw my pay. Sailors were paid once every two weeks. The sub was to tide me over until my documents caught up with my next ship. At the Regulating Office, only the Leading Regulator was sufficiently interested in answering any of my queries.

"It says here *at Portsmouth*," he said, looking at my draft chit, "so it must be."

I was beginning to think it was all some kind of conspiracy, punishment perhaps for losing my 'pot and brush, painting for the use of.' I thought that there may have been some collusion between the PO of the Side Party and the Regulating Office and I was being sent on a humiliating wild goose chase. I thought that by now they were all probably looking at their watches or out of windows at me, scuttling around looking for a ship that did not exist and telephoning the next place I was sent to, to keep massaging the joke. Crossing the parade ground, on my way back to the accommodation block, I ran into an ex-shipmate from HMS *Solebay*. He was hobbling along on crutches as he had fallen into a dry dock a couple of months before and broken his leg. Unfortunately, the fracture had then developed complications and they had to re-break it and set it again. He was still on sick parade.

"Hey Shiner," I called after him. "Ever heard of the *Rampart*?" He stopped and looked around.

"Ah, Dickie Barr, it's you," he replied. Then shaking his head, "No, what is it?"

"I've no idea mate, I was hoping you might be able to throw some light on it."

He looked at the ground for a moment before replying,

"It could be one of those new frigates, I think they are called 'Leanders.' I read in the *Navy News* that they are just now being introduced."

"Yeah, you could be right. It's probably so new that no-one's ever heard of it," I said, brightening up.

"When are you joining anyway?" he continued.

"Tomorrow, mate,' I chirped.

"Christ alive, that's some pier head jump isn't it?" he returned, rather indelicately and looking astonished.

"Thanks shipmate," I muttered.

"Any idea where I might find it?"

"Nah mate," he shook his head, "but careful who you ask. An oppo of mine was busting for a piss and asked a Dockyard Matey if he knew where the urinal was. All he got was, "Dunno, how many funnels has it got?" and with that, he hobbled away. I stood looking after him for a while, thinking, *Yes, what is all the rush about?*

That evening I packed my kit and chatted to the few chaps around that I knew in the vast accommodation block that had served as my home for four months but none of them could help me locate either the type or whereabouts of my new ship.

3.   An Excursion to Scarborough

Dockyard Matey's Ditty

Descending to my mess one day aboard this grand old ship,
I found a Dockyard Matey asleep upon my kit.
He looked for all the world like he was going to give me gyp,
And growled, "Why are you looking at me?"
I said "Well in your overalls, you really look a scruff."
He said, "I've have to work today and life is really tough.
I'd rather stay here kipping but there isn't time enough,
Cos I'm tired and I'm off for tea."

Richard Barr

By 9am the next morning I had taken breakfast, returned my bedding and, with all the boxes on my leaving card fully stamped and signed, I crossed the parade ground to the Regulating Office. There I exchanged the card for my joining instructions and a large, sealed, brown paper envelope. It was a cold, bright, sunny start to the day and I felt extremely light of heart. Close by there were parked a number of grey wooden handcarts, each with a pair of bowed shafts. They looked like the sort of thing a donkey would feel at home between but these had been used in Nelson's days for moving stores, sails, cordage and the like around the old naval yards. The few that still remained were used by sailors to transport kit and hammocks or indeed anything else that was either too bulky or too heavy to carry personally, yet was not big or heavy enough to warrant the use of a *utilicon* (van) or a lorry. The two large spoked wheels were about five feet in diameter, leaving the axle maybe two and a half feet or more off the ground. The distance between the two wheels was also about five feet. Made of wood, they were reasonably lightweight and of the most pleasing shape to behold. Pulling one out, I re-crossed the parade ground to where I had left my kitbag, suitcase and grip. On the way there, I stopped for several moments by the cinder training area to watch a Field Gun Crew being put through its paces. I thought to myself that I would like to have a go at that at some time in the future.

With everything in the world that I owned loaded aboard the cart, I stepped between the shafts and started the journey to join my new ship and whatever fate awaited me. Passing down the line of old Victorian accommodation blocks, with the memories they held, I remember thinking, 'I hope that this is the last time I see this place,' little realising that I would do so twice more in the years ahead.

It is always a strange sensation leaving a ship and those you have come to know intimately and trust explicitly, for possibly the last time. It is a feeling that never deserted me, nor many others that I knew. Though feeling light of heart as I trundled the cart out through the main gate and on to the road, I felt it yet again, not as acutely as on other occasions, I confess, given that barracks was a large impersonal place and my stay there had been but a relatively short one.

Leaving a ship and its company that had been closely knitted together for two years or more, however, was another matter altogether. All that you had come to know and understand, the idiosyncrasies of those amongst whom you lived, worked and played alongside, the sheer familiarity of all around you, would be shattered overnight. All would have to be painstakingly rebuilt again from the bottom up in some other place, and in another community. I truly felt the loss of leaving my early ships more greatly than I did of leaving my family home for the first time. It was for me, as a youngster, a time of great apprehension.

In a thoughtful mood, I turned left outside the main gate and five hundred yards further on, left again heading for Unicorn Gate, the nearest entry to the dockyard. There was a lot of traffic about, mostly on foot and bicycle, much of it heading to and from the dockyard. Thousands were based in ships of the fleet and several thousand more were employed within the dockyard's confines. At this time of the day the flow of humanity into the yard was immense.

In the 1950s and 60s Portsmouth Naval Dockyard was a vast sprawling maze of roadways, tramways, jetties, dry docks, non-tidal and tidal basins, heavy workshops, storehouses, store compounds, sail lofts, rope walks, chain stores and offices, covering several square miles. To walk unencumbered from one end to the other could take you well over an hour if you knew, and were able to take, the shortest route. For a stranger, unsure of his bearings, it could take several hours. Very often, the intended route would be temporarily blocked due to ship movements in or out of dry docks or basins, resulting in long and frustrating detours.

It could be particularly frustrating if you could see the object of your mission just a few hundred yards away across the water but with the connecting caisson removed. If searching for a particular berth or jetty, it was a relatively simple task to look it up on the plans displayed inside the various entry-exit gates and navigate your way there. If, like me, you were searching for a ship of which you knew nothing but its name, did not know its whereabouts, and whom no one else appeared to know anything at all, then it was always likely to be a tiresome search. And so it turned out.

Shoving and pushing my way through the throng, I came up to the giant Dockyard Gates. Here I showed my identity card to the dockyard policeman and asked, "Where may I find the *Rampart* please?"

"Rampart? Rampart? Hmm..." he muttered thoughtfully, and then, calling through the gate office window, "Hey Sid, what berth is *Rampart* on?"

There was silence for a full half minute or more, by which time he had become engaged in sorting out someone else's enquiry. After what seemed an eternity from inside came a voice,

"I know she's in, Stan, coz she was in the ship movement orders on Monday. Try the coaling jetty."

"Cheers mate!" I threw back. Ah ha! I thought, that sounds better, much better. But wait a minute, the coaling jetty? That didn't sound altogether healthy to me. What would a gleaming new Leander class frigate be doing at the old coaling jetty? I thought all coal-burning ships had long since been discarded. Little by little, I had secretly begun to doubt the Leander concept, which had, it must be conceded, fairly tenuous legitimacy in any case. With directions to the coaling jetty firmly cemented in my head, I climbed again between the shafts and stepped out with gusto, nearly knocking a Dockyard Matey off his bicycle in the process.

"Watch where you're going you dozy arsehole!" he grumbled, not bothering to look up as he cycled on. I was about to respond but thought better of it, not wishing to cause a scene right in front of the dockyard police. I did make a mental note of the yellow and blue bike he was riding though, just in case I came across it on my travels that day. I would have my revenge if I did. If that could be called my first setback of the day, I encountered my second before I had travelled a further hundred yards or more. Tramways! The yard was criss-crossed with them, like spaghetti on a platter, not all of them headed the way that I wanted to go. The handcart, though not particularly heavy, developed a mind of its own and a stubbornness that thwarted my every effort at forward motion. Time and again I hauled it this way, only to find it wanted to go that way, as one wheel or the other dropped into a tramway groove. One handicap I quickly discovered was that the thickness of the wheels was, much the same as that of the grooves that they fell into. Getting the wheels out of them had me cursing and sweating. I felt and probably looked like a demented donkey on scrumpy.

My next handicap was that of visibility. The old Victorian workshop and stores buildings, stacked Portacabins, numerous cranes and ships superstructures were so tall, and the roadways so narrow in comparison, that most of the time I could see only that which lay directly ahead of me, or, at junctions to right and left.

In addition, there were lorries of every description belching clouds of blue black smoke, vans, cars and cyclists too, all competing for right of way. Finally there were the Dockyard Mateys themselves, multitudes of them, clad in beige overalls, tramping along in all directions, some carrying bits of equipment, others with toolboxes and most with nothing at all but vacant expressions on their faces, for all the world as if they were on a day excursion to Scarborough. Fellow sailors returning from the night ashore completed this perplexing potpourri. It reminded me of match day at St Andrews football stadium when the gates opened and disgorged the hordes out onto the streets after a match. As I threaded my erratic course between them, it struck me that the whole of the dockyard was on the move.

Dockyard Mateys exhibited an air of superior indifference to us matelots. They behaved as if the yard and its contents belonged to them. Times for starting and completing tasks were their prerogative. They were disinclined to move aside and make way for you, so you had to negotiate a path around them. When your ship went into dockyard hands for refit or maintenance, Dockyard Mateys laid siege to it. They invaded it like ants, trailed cables, airlines and hoses over hallowed decks and along busy passageways. They descended into your mess deck, *your living room,* and once there, they settled down to make themselves at home, opened their lunch boxes and denied you a seat at your own meal table. They were everywhere you didn't want them to be and nowhere to be found when you needed them. Consequently, we hated going into dockyard hands.

Dockyard Mateys and sailors have had a love/hate relationship for years and both sides are used to it. I must confess, though, that I knew many whom I later worked alongside, who were genuinely good guys. Equally, a friend of mine once heard a senior dockyard official suggest to an officer that, "If only your ships would stay at sea, the Dockyard would run more smoothly!"

But at the time they were most disobliging. Before the day was out, I am certain that I saw the same individuals wandering around doing much the same things as when I had first spotted them earlier that day. One guy in particular stood out; he had a large beard and was wearing a baseball cap (unusual in those days) and carrying on his shoulder a length of metal tubing. I first spotted him shortly after my brush with the grumpy cyclist. An hour or so later I had hauled my cart as far as the coaling jetty, which, incidentally, faced out towards Whale Island, the *Alma Mater* of the Gunnery Branch. Its hallowed parade ground had been the chessboard for a thousand and one fully booted and gaitered Gunnery Instructors and hordes of drilling naval ratings down the years. I fancied I could hear those GI's voices drifting over the water above the noise and hubbub of the dockyard, conducting their charges from one square to another. It was there that I espied the 'metal tube carrier' for the second time that day. He was wandering along, seemingly quite aimlessly, whistling to himself. I nodded in his direction but he did not acknowledge my presence.

The Old Coaling Jetty was just that ... old. The quay was where generations of ships had berthed to 'coal ship' but with the introduction of oil fuel, it had fallen into almost total disuse. But all the signs were there to remind one of its history; grime, buildings blackened by years of exposure to coal dust, railway detritus, coal hoppers and the like. To my utter delight, however, there I beheld a ship. I could not make out its name as it was bows-on but I could discern its inelegant appearance. It had a strange bow shape, a little like you would see on an ice breaker, and a rather tall, ungainly funnel. Likening it to an ugly duckling, I crossed to it and was not wholly disappointed to read HMS *Plover* inscribed on its ceremonial lifebelt. It was a minelayer and furthermore it was a coal burner.

"Do you know where *Rampart* is mate?" I called to what I took to be the QM (Quartermaster) manning the gangway. The figure stepped forward from beneath the sea boat blowing into his hands.

"Och, It was just astern of us the day afore yesterday, yin," he replied, in a thick Glaswegian accent. Looking towards the empty space astern, he continued. "It was gaen though when I came on watch yesterday afternoon."

"Any idea where?" I threw back at him. He shrugged non-committally and returned to his refuge.

"Thanks anyway," I muttered, turning back to where I had left my gear. I tramped on toward Excellent Steps and the warmth of the dockside canteen there.

It was nearly ten thirty and I was in need of sustenance and a moment's rest. When I arrived there, the place was thick with matelots, dockyard mateys and smoke in roughly equal proportions, including the 'metal tube carrier.' His tubing was standing in a corner next to where he was in deep conversation with two other dockies.

This canteen was one of several dotted about the yard and used by all-comers. It sold hot tea, coffee and chocolate and a pretty good selection of pies and sandwiches. I never went there but it was crammed to capacity and more often than not, I had to stand to eat and drink. The tables were always full with mateys, most of them being sat there when I entered and still there when I left. I wondered more than once if this was the waiting room for the excursion to Scarborough. After finishing off my mug of hot tea, I was glad to extricate myself and to exchange some stale woodbine smoke for fresh air.

I spent the rest of the morning combing the jetties and basins at the north-eastern end of the yard where, traditionally, small ships were berthed. I had come to the conclusion some time earlier that *Rampart*, by its obscurity, was not going to be a big ship, a Leander still a vague possibility, but not a big ship. Each one that I came upon, whether in the basins or dry-docks, I checked out. There were frigates and boom- defence boats, tugs, destroyers, submarines and minesweepers, but no *Rampart*. By two o'clock, still shipless and feeling well and truly knackered, I found myself back at Excellent Steps canteen. Once inside, I collapsed with another mug of tea, four large pasties (I was famished by then) and a used copy of the *Daily Mirror* that had been left behind by someone. The dockyard having returned to work after lunch at one thirty, meant that the canteen had thinned out a bit. But the metal tube was still propped up in a corner whilst its owner's head was now stuck in a copy of *Sporting Life*.

What a life! I thought. Over lunch I glanced idly at my horoscope. It read: *'You are going through a period of change in your life, be prepared for early setbacks, your star is in the ascendancy...'* or some such crap. I have never read another since. On asking around amongst the few inhabitants and smokers for information on the possible whereabouts of the good ship *Rampart*, I drew another complete blank. It was becoming depressing.

That afternoon, with a slight drizzle beginning to fall, my cart was in collision with a dockyard apprentice. I say 'in collision' to cover my embarrassment. I had left the canteen and was making my way towards Kings Stairs. Upon looking over my shoulder to make sure I was not about to be run down as I crossed a busy junction, I was flabbergasted to find all five feet nothing of the cheeky sod sat in my cart, hitching a ride. In the time it took me to pull up, drop the shafts so as get near enough to shove his monkey wrench up his backside, he had vaulted nimbly over the back board and was lost to sight in the sea of beige-clad mateys with blank faces, excursioning to Scarborough.

"Bloody cheeky little sod!" I shouted to no one in particular, venting my frustration rather than any feeling of malice. I actually smiled inwardly at the sauce of the fellow. By a half past five, I was up near the main gate and the big ships.

I had passed beneath the *Albion*, waving to my ex-shipmates as I did so, and crossed the basin to where the carrier *Triumph* was undergoing conversion. There being no sign of my ship, I retraced my steps to South Railway Jetty and had come upon the colossal bulk of the 42,000-ton battleship *Vanguard*. She dwarfed just about everything else in sight and blotted out the horizon ahead of me. I rested for a short while to take in this awesome sight.

'Awesome' has become a well-worn adjective, used these days to describe just about anything that occurs outside of the day to day drudgery of modern life. Britain's last remaining battleship was truly awesome, in the intended sense of the word, when seen from where I stood. Gigantic, majestic, graceful yet immensely powerful and menacing were just a few of the words that I could use to describe her. I marvelled at the massive gun turrets in their barbettes and wondered just what it must feel like to be inside them for the ratings of the 'then there is also, of course, the Gunnery Branch' when those things went off bang.

Her crewmembers on deck looked Lilliputian beside her towering superstructure and secondary armament and I wondered idly to myself how it would be impossible not to get lost in such a vast ship. Her liberty men, in uniform, were fallen in on her foredeck being inspected prior to embarking upon an evening's liberty ashore. Eventually, with the inspection complete, they were fallen out of line and came tumbling down her forward gangway, hurrying off towards the main gate. Some of them would probably be heading to their homes, wives and children, others for sport or recreational perhaps, and the remainder, probably to the local hostelries and sailors' rests.

Glancing around me, I observed that the dockyard in general was by now emptying fast. Having read every name on every ship in the place, I was convinced that *Rampart* had gone to sea without me. *Where does that leave me now?* I thought earnestly. *Possibly absent without leave, or, worse still, failed to arrive on board in time for sailing.* That was an offence punishable by a spell in detention quarters. But then, how was I to have known that she was sailing that day? My brain was becoming tired and addled. Trudging on after the throng for a while, I then did that which I have always done when faced with failure or defeat. I became belligerent.

"Fuck the *Rampart* and fuck the Navy as well!" I shouted aloud but, fortunately for me, not loud enough for those within earshot to hear. Anyway, from what I could see, they appeared to be far too busy hurrying home from work or from their exhausting day out at Scarborough to be inconvenienced by my plight. *Well!* I thought, *what am I to do? I can't go back to barracks, I don't belong there anymore. There is only one thing for it...*

With that, I turned on my heel, turned my back on the *Vanguard* and trekked back the way I had come. By now I knew the route like the back of my hand and was alongside Unicorn Gate for the second time that day by 7pm. I kept a wary eye out for the 'metal tube carrier' but never set eyes upon him again. Also, in my earnest desire to find my ship, I had completely forgotten to look out for the yellow and blue bicycle I had met with earlier in the day. Had I spotted it at that moment, it would have gone into the harbour. My pleading with the dockyard police to allow me to leave my kitbag and case at the gate until morning was met sympathetically. Thereafter I viewed the dockyard police almost with affection. With just my Burberry and grip, I walked the two hundred yards or so to Aggie Weston's Royal Sailors Rest, just off Commercial Road, and purchased a bed for the night for five shillings. I did not have the stomach for a night out at the rather more licentious hostelries such as the Sussex, Albany or Lennox.

Dame Agnes Weston's Royal Sailors Rests were established by royal charter in all the major naval ports, through the endeavours of that august lady, to provide a safe haven ashore for sailors on leave from their ships, as well as catering for their spiritual needs. Besides providing food, accommodation and recreational activities, they also provided the opportunity for sailors to find peace, quiet and if desired, spiritual comfort. In all the times I ever lodged at an Aggie Weston's I met truly nice, kind and helpful people, fellow lodgers as well as staff. Collecting my key with its gigantic fob, I trudged two floors up to my 4ft by 8ft room with its green walls, linoleum floor, single iron bed and bedside locker. It represented a place in heaven to me just then. Hanging my Burberry up to dry, I collapsed onto the bed and fell into a deep sleep.

I was rudely awakened by a door banging further down the corridor and glanced with a bleary eye at my watch. Nine thirty. Time, if I am very lucky, to get down to the canteen for a mug of cocoa and a sticky bun. Such was the sum total of my desires at that moment. The canteen was rather tired and dreary looking, as though in need of a refit. It was also fairly devoid of human life. Along one wall was a counter with one or two plates of buns or scones upon it. Behind it was a rack containing *nutty* (chocolates and sweets), an empty hot display cabinet, a hot water boiler and a doorway through into the kitchen. The rest of the open space was taken up by tables and chairs, perhaps twelve tables in all. Sat around one table were five or six fellow sailors, the sole occupants of the canteen, *due, most likely, to it being a non-pay week,* I thought to myself. There were signs of it having been fairly busier earlier that evening, judging by the number of tables that there were littered with dirty mugs and plates.

The middle-aged lady behind the counter was 'awfully sorry' but the kitchen was closed. She would make me a sandwich though, if I so desired. Clutching my mug and the cheese and tomato sandwich, there being no sticky buns left, I went over and sat at a cleared table close to where the other occupants were seated. I was intent only on eating and drinking my fare before turning in. I had blisters the size of half crowns on my hands and my feet felt like they had been spit char grilled. Some while later some of the occupants of the other table began to drift off until there were just two remaining. One of these was a rather tall and gangly two badge Leading Signalman *(Bunting Tossser)* who was a good deal older than me but whom I had noticed glancing in my direction from time to time. Eventually, he turned his head and said casually, "You don't mind my saying but you look a bit pissed off, old chum."

I looked across to where the voice came from and met his gaze, then returned nonchalantly, "You can say that again." trying not to put too much emphasis on looking pissed off.

"Your party hasn't ditched you has she?" he continued.

"No, not at all. Ship problems," I countered. "I've been looking for a ship called *Rampart* since ten this morning and I am just about shagged out."

At this, his *oppo* (opposite number or chum) who, until that moment had been totally ensconced in reading his magazine, suddenly looked first in my direction and then back to his friend and said quietly, Rampart... isn't that the thing tied up alongside of us, Jonah?"

Jonah paused for a second or two, then nodded at him and turned again to me, smiling. "Yeah, *Rampart* is berthed alongside of us."

"Alongside of what?" I said, astonished, spilling the last dregs of cocoa down my white front.

"The *Vanguard*," he said, "on South Railway jetty."

I was speechless for as long as it took for me to recall that I had stood admiring this great ship just that very afternoon.

"I know where the fucking *Vanguard* is," I blurted out, "but, I never saw *Rampart* today."

Jonah's oppo responded. "Well you probably wouldn't have done. It's lashed up outboard of us and it's only a farty little tank landing craft anyway."

I was totally gobsmacked. The pair of them must have thought me deranged. I sat staring at them for what seemed an age, not knowing what to do or say. I was so happy I nearly shit myself. At a single stroke, when I had least expected it, I had not only discovered the whereabouts of my lost ship but, in the same breath, had heard it described as 'only a farty little tank landing craft.' From my mouth emitted forth a meek, 'What?' and to myself under by breath *a landing craft?*

My brain went into paralysis again. Not a gleaming new Leander then, but a *landing craft*. I thought, Le-an-der. La-nd-ing and then dismissed the notion; no it was not remotely similar. It did not help the situation having never actually seen either type of ship before. I could not get a mental picture in my mind.

"Cheers oppo, I'll sleep lighter tonight," I said, and scuttled off before they could enlighten me any further on this 'farty little landing craft'. I felt their stares follow me as I left. They, no doubt thinking, that I had been bevvying up in the Albany or the Lennox.

It took me ages to get to sleep that night. Not a new sleek Leander then but a 'farty little tank landing craft.' What would I be actually doing on a 'farty little tank landing craft' anyway? I thought that they belonged to the army. Maybe that was it! No wonder no one had been able to help me. I was being seconded to the army! That must be why nobody had been able to answer any of my questions, and God knows, I had asked enough people. My imagination ran wild until at last, in the early wee hours, sleep came to my rescue and a curtain of darkness descended upon my tormented horizon.

I was out of bed, washed, fed and on my way through the same light drizzle towards the dockyard gate by 7am. There, I was re-acquainted with my cart and collected my gear. By 8am. I was again standing alongside Vanguard, at the bottom of the for'ard gangway, which led up onto the foredeck of the enormous ship, slightly abaft of B turret. Waiting for a gap in the human traffic boarding her, I heaved my kitbag onto my shoulder and, grabbing my case and grip in the other hand, I toiled upwards towards the brow. It seemed like miles. Stepping gingerly onto the gleaming white, scrubbed deck, I approached the QM.

"I'm looking for HMS Rampart *hooky* (leading hand),' I said, showing him my identity card.

Looking me up and down, he replied, "Over there, starboard side, aft of B Turret," indicating the direction I should take. I saluted the officer of the day as best I was able under my burden and set forth forward to round the front of A Turret and cross to the other side of the ship.

'How fortunate am I,' I mused, as I wandered forward in a world of my own, 'to be on the hallowed teak deck of this famous ship.' I had read all about her in the *Boys Own* magazine many years before. In reality, of course, *Vanguard* had not been completed until 1946, after the end of hostilities, and so had not actually seen action in any of the great sea battles of the Second World War, but she was the largest and the last British battleship, a symbol of our former greatness and all that I felt proud to be a part of.

On rounding the front of A Turret I was stopped dead in my tracks by a shriek that detonated inside my brain and shattered my composure.

"You there! Yes you! The scrawny little git with the kit bag! Get off my foc's'le now – AT THE DOUBLE!"

I looked around, startled, to see a wall of ratings, maybe thirty or so, in line abreast with their trousers rolled up to their knees, wielding long handled scrubbing brushes, advancing towards me from the bow of the ship. In their van, holding a hosepipe spewing seawater, standing with his legs wide astride, was a fearsome Chief Petty Officer. I could clearly see the veins of wrath standing out from his temples.

In the time it took for my brain to register this picture, it had also somehow connected the voice with its owner. I stopped, started, stopped again, stared and finally legged it, all in one lissom movement. I didn't stop until I was out of his sight down the starboard side and had reached the vertical ladder hanging down to the deck of what I took to be the *Rampart* far below. I felt weak at the knees through exertion and stung by my feeble reaction. 'I must learn to become more assertive,' I thought.

Anyway, once there, I attached with a snap hook, my kitbag, case and grip to a *Handy Billy* (lightweight block and tackle) and, pausing only long enough to make sure no one was ascending, hoisted them over the rail and lowered them just short of the speed of gravity to the deck below.

Glancing back, to make sure I was not being pursued, I quickly followed them down. A long, long way down.

On stepping onto the green painted iron deck of the *Rampart* the first things I was aware of were twilight and silence. Twilight because daylight was almost blotted from view by the towering cathedral alongside; silence because not a sound assailed my ears, nothing. Not a soul moved. Getting my bearings, I gingerly picked up my kit and made my way aft, to where I thought the accommodation could be. Poking my head through the only open doorway, I climbed inside and entered a narrow passageway that led directly across the ship, leading to a similar door opening on to the deck on the other side. Halfway along this, were two other passageways, one leading forward for about 5 meters and the other aft roughly double that distance.

At this point, looking forward and facing me, was a door marked *Junior Ratings Mess*. To its right was another marked *Senior Ratings Mess* and to the left, the *Coxswain's Office*. This door was open and led into a cabin with a bunk with a writing bureau beneath it. The cabin was empty. Looking aft, I could see bathrooms and *heads* (toilets) to the left and the galley to the right. One ladder led down to a compartment marked *Troop's Messdeck* and another upwards to the wardroom, wardroom cabins, charthouse, wheelhouse and bridge. A further ladder descended though a hatch to the engine room. That seemed about it. After the *Albion* it was positively pokey.

Yet, apart from there being no one about, there was no doubting the fact that this was a ship commissioned in the Royal Navy. It was spotlessly clean and in every way shipshape and Bristol Fashion. I was just a little unnerved at there being no-one around for me to announce my arrival to, particularly as to my mind I was already a day late. Secondly, I was a little too timid to just throw open the door and enter the Junior Ratings Mess. Checking to make sure that I was not mistaken and that no one was out and about, I eventually sat down on my kitbag beside the galley door and waited for something to happen. As always, wait long enough and it does. And when it did, it was worth waiting for.

First, I heard a thud on the deck about where I had landed, announcing the arrival of someone else. There followed heavy footsteps advancing towards the door through which I had entered. Seconds later, framed in the doorway, stood a grey haired, iron faced, three badge leading seaman, clad in white hat, greatcoat and white silk scarf. He surveyed me for a moment without speaking and I intuitively recognised him as a senior seaman in the ship. With a quick nod and an authoritative 'Wait there a moment whacker' to me, he strode purposefully towards the door marked *Junior Ratings Mess*, entered through it and crashed it closed behind him. Until that moment, I thought I had heard all the natty 'Wakey Wakey rise and shine the morning's fine' compilations used for calling the hands that there possibly were, but what followed that morning was an education for me. No known expletive or humorous epithet was missed out. Every swear word I had ever heard was used. Every orifice in the human body and what might happen to it if its owner was still horizontal in five seconds, was described in lurid detail. It was classic and it was delivered in a broad scouse accent. No mother of any one of the occupants therein would have wanted to have been witness to the horoscopes read to their sons that morning in the junior ratings mess aboard HMS *Rampart*. The comments would have shaken their sensibilities to the core.

Within seconds, pandemonium had broken loose.

The door was flung open again and, one after the other, the bleary-eyed occupants spilled out, some naked, others with only a towel wrapped around them, clutching toothbrushes and soap boxes and heading for the bathroom and heads. I counted seven or eight before the Leading Hand reappeared, with a glint in his eye and the first signs of a grin creasing his weatherbeaten face.

He crossed to where I was stood and said with a grin, "Eeerh, call me 'Scouse', and who are you shipmate?"

"Able Seaman Barr, hooky," I replied, and handing him the envelope, added, "Here are my joining instructions."

"Eeerh, right, at last, we were expecting you yesterday." Looking at my kitbag just outside the galley door, he continued, "You must be the new seaman cook, welcome aboard."

I stared at him for a moment, unable to comprehend the significance of his last statement.

"No, no, no, you don't understand. I am a seaman, not a sea-man cook, look here, look at my joining instructions, you must be pulling my leg," I retorted.

"I most certainly am not," responded Scouse, the hint of a smile not having left his face. "Now that you are here, and for the next six months at least, your part of ship will be cook's mate and I know that you will enjoy it. Oh, and don't worry," he added, "You will have plenty of opportunity to practice your seamanship. You will still keep watches with the rest of the seamen in the ship."

With his tirade of just a few moments before in the Junior Ratings' Mess still ringing in my ears, I decided to let the matter rest there.

Indicating towards the troop mess deck accommodation, he said, "For the time being, I suggest to get your gear below, take any cot and locker you like, there is no-one else down there, change into the rig of the day and report back to me an hour from now.

4. Westward Ho!

From *Desperation*

While on my way to Devon,
My pace was getting wider,
My eyes were glazed, my speech was slurred,
My breath smelled strongly of cider.
My feet seemed three feet off the ground,
My arms were swinging round me,
And the birds were flying upside down,
Which really did astound me.

  N Art Bruen

Having changed, unpacked and stowed my kit as instructed, I went and reported to Scouse, the Leading Hand, who showed me to the galley, where several others and I helped ourselves to breakfast, my second of the day. I found that in *Rampart* this activity was standard practice when in harbour. The Leading Cook left the raw materials in the fridge the night before and the ship's company helped themselves as they pleased the following morning. The Wardroom Steward and Senior Ratings Mess Man looked after the needs of their respective messes. I was informed that everyone was trusted to leave the galley spotless on completion. After breakfast, Scouse took me on a tour of the ship. At about eleven thirty the Leading Cook and the *Swain* (Coxswain) appeared at the rail of HMS *Vanguard* above. They had with them a variety of victuals, purchased ashore that morning. Scouse told me to go and lend them a hand. Using the simple pulley system, aptly named a *Handy Billy,* with which I had lowered my kit to the deck, I and two other fellows lowered these stores from the deck of *Vanguard* to the port walkway where they were sorted, some being brought directly to the galley while the remainder was taken down to the provision store. On completion, I went aft to the galley, where I introduced myself to the Leading Cook, who was busy unpacking boxes and bags as I stepped through the door.

"Leading Cook, I think that I am your new assistant," I said.

After eyeing me up and down for a few moments, as if deciding whether or not he really wanted me as his 'mate', he replied, "So *you* drew the short straw did you?"

The irony of that remark was lost on me for a minute or two. Only much later did I find out that, before my arrival, straws had been drawn for this duty and my name had been on one of them. I guess that the straw with my name on it must have been returned to the draw.

Leading Cook 'Dolly' Gray was an unassuming, conscientious and very competent ship's cook. He was also a very patient tutor. He had one glaring deficiency in his constitution, however; he became chronically seasick the moment the ship hit a bit of rough weather. Most seamen never suffer from this debilitating problem. There are some for whom a few days at sea is required in order to re-establish their sea legs following a spell on dry land and a few who resort to anti-seasickness tablets but only a tiny minority, God help them, suffer intolerably and for them there is no known cure. Poor 'Dolly' was one of the latter. Try as he might, he could not overcome the problem. It is said that sea-sickness comes in three phases: first, you think you are going to die; next, you hope that you *are* going to die; then comes the awful realization that you are *not* going to die; and after that you get better. The only certain cure for sea-sickness is to sit under a tree.

Even as we were singling up mooring lines and preparing to leave harbour, Dolly would be rushing around, giving me my instructions regarding what to do should he have to absent himself in a hurry.

But as I stood before him that day, I knew nothing of the Leading Cook's predilection to seasickness. He and I got on famously from the first moment. Within days, under his careful and assiduous guidance, I learned to cut vegetables precisely and expeditiously, without adding the end of my finger to the pile, to break eggs with one hand without breaking the yolks as well, to mix and bake pastry and *scabby babies heads* (suet puddings made with steak and kidney, much loved by sailors) to make stock, duchess potatoes, *figgy duff* (sultana or date pudding, sometimes referred to as 'belly timber' due to its robust and filling nature) and much more besides. I was taught when to start different dishes, how to stagger them through the oven or put them on the hotplate so that they would be ready for serving at the same time. A steep learning curve that was to stand me in good stead in later years.

On the lower deck of the Royal Navy at that time, there were two types of messing: *Broadside* and *Canteen*. Broadside messing was the norm in medium and large ships. These ships were victualed directly from the various naval victualing yards, either while alongside in port or at sea via sea transfer from a stores ship. Smaller ships, within what was loosely termed *Coastal Forces* were permitted to receive a monetary allowance and establish accounts with accredited civilian suppliers ashore. This was known as *Canteen Messing*. It was more practical for them, given that storage space in small ships was always at a premium and it was not always cost effective for victualing yards to send small quantities of supplies around the country by road or rail. *Rampart* belonged to the latter group.

The Navigator held the purse strings and the Swain kept the accounts. In liaison with the Leading Cook and the Wardroom Mess Steward, the Swain decided the priorities and proceeded ashore to purchase or order for delivery, our daily food rations. Also, these were the days before the introduction of dining halls and cafeterias, except in the case of the most modern aircraft carriers. In all other ships, food was prepared by each mess in turn, who took whatever they had concocted to the galley for cooking, baking or just plain murdering. Each mess in the ship ran a roster, whereby, for a twenty-four hour period, commencing at 0800 each day and on a rotating basis, two of us ratings assumed the duty of *Cooks of the Mess*. Between 0800 and

0930 we cleared up after breakfast, scrubbed out, then collected vegetables from the cold store, meat from the beef screen, then sugar, butter, bread, tea and milk from the dry store, according to the number of men in the mess. The galley issued a daily menu and the Cooks of the Mess prepared the vegetables and meat accordingly, down in each of the messes. When completed, the prepared food was placed in clearly marked trays, taken up to the galley and left for the cooks to cook. Our cooks' tasks completed, we carried on with our normal duties.

At 1145 each day, the pipe *Cooks of the Mess to clean* was made. This was the signal for us to stop what we were doing, wash and clean and prepare the mess tables for dinner. At 1155, the pipe *Cooks of the Mess to the Galley* was made. This was the call for us to return to the galley, collect the trays that we had prepared earlier and take them back down into the mess, where as many as twenty or thirty hungry mouths were ready to devour the contents.

'Cooks of the Mess' usually had to withstand a lot of good natured chaff and barracking from messmates, all of whom, until it was their turn, believed that they could do the job better. Only a few years earlier, 'Cooks of the Mess' also had to prepare the *duff* (pudding) besides the main course. This task, however, was now undertaken by the ship's cooks. After dinner, we cleared away the tables, washed the plates, cutlery and trays in the mess fanny, cleared up spillage and ditched the gash. On completion, it was time to turn-to again, so no time for relaxation. The same process was repeated at supper time, 1830, except that the ships' cooks prepared all the food. The following morning at 0700, we collected breakfast and that concluded our twenty-four hour spell of domestic duty. It was also customary for us Cooks of the Mess to provide from our own sources the washing powder for washing up after meals, usually *Daz* or *Persil* purchased from the ship's canteen or *NAAFI*, as it was better known. Carrying four or five trays of hot food safely from the galley to the mess often called for meticulous timing, perfect balance and immense good fortune. This was particularly so when negotiating the heaving deck of a destroyer in heavy seas and the near vertical ladders down to the mess decks below.

Once, in HMS *Solebay*, I staggered the length of the ship in a moderately rough sea, with three trays, laden with meat and three vegetables. As I arrived at the ladder leading down to my mess, I overbalanced and dropped the lot on top of my oppo, who was halfway up the ladder waiting to receive them from me. I will never forget the explosion of fury from below, as long as I draw breath. It is amusing to relate this tale long afterwards but it was a catastrophe at the time. The following week, during the ship's weekly quiz, one of the twenty questions was 'Who is the most unpopular person in a naval warship?' Every one of the eight 'junior rates' messes answered 'Ordinary Seaman Barr!' I was made Cook of the Mess for the following seven days for my pains.

But I was not the only one to have a mishap like this. A stoker from the after stokers mess one day lost the whole of his burden overboard when he was swept by a *goffa* [incoming sea] into the scuppers. At least in my case we were able to scrape the remains of the dinner off the deck to feed the hungry. Not so the stokers mess, God bless them. Like me that day, they had to go without.

In *Rampart*, because there was a cook's mate allocated full time, the Cooks of the Mess had only to collect cooked food from the galley, take it back to the mess and then clear up on completion. The only time this routine altered was when troops were embarked.

The Leading Cook's susceptibility to seasickness put me in mind of the first and only time that I ever suffered that curse. Two years previously, prior to commissioning HMS *Solebay*, we, the members of the ship's 'then there is also, of course, the Gunnery Branch' put to sea in the Portland sea training ship HMS *Vigo* for gunnery practice. I was allocated the task of star shell operator, my action station for the next two years. My position in the enclosed 4ft 5in turret was right down at the front, squeezed in just below its twin barrels. To reach this position, I had to enter the turret through a tiny hole from the gun bay, as opposed to the door at the rear of the turret by which the rest of the crew entered. The gun bay was situated one deck below the turret. Once in my place, there was no way out until the turret ceased revolving, was trained fore and aft again and then locked into position on completion of the shoot. With the stark warning, 'If you are only halfway through hole and the turret revolves, you will be sliced in two' firmly embedded as a vivid picture within my mind, I scrambled up and in, like a pine marten up a tree.

With my earphones clamped firmly on my head, I awaited instructions, for I could see very little beyond the dials and wheels in front of me and the position was totally claustrophobic. Once outside Portland breakwater, the ship headed into a good long swell and before long, we were bouncing up and down quite sickeningly.

I could hear the shouts of the Captain-of-the-Gun, just above and to the rear of me, as he responded to the Gunnery Officer's orders, which were relayed over the turret loudspeaker from the Transmitting Station (TS) two decks below.

"Testing circuits," followed by "Load with starshell," came the voice from the TS.

"Load with starshell, load, load, load!" repeated the Captain-of-the- Gun. This is where I jumped into life and played my little part, or didn't, as became the case. My task was to set the fuse on each shell, so that it would explode at the correct height over the intended target, thereby illuminating it. This was done quite simply, by marrying up the pointers on the dial in front of me, using the little brass wheels provided. As the pointer from the TS moved round on the dial, to indicate a certain range or height required, I turned the wheels frantically left or right, following it with my own pointer, thereby adjusting the fuse on the tip of the shells as I did so. Eventually, the Captain of the Gun reported, "Both guns loaded, ready to fire."

'Clang-clang!' went the answering gong, indicating that the firing circuits had been closed. After a brief moment, the voice from the TS responded, "Shoot!"

Then there was silence, whilst everybody mentally prepared themselves for the crash to follow. When it came, it was like a crack of thunder, amplified beyond disco club proportions by tenfold or more. The noise reverberated around my brain for what seemed a lifetime. Everyone in the turret had ear defenders on, except me; I had the headphones. Why, I never found out, no-one ever spoke to me through them.

Clang! Went the empty brass cordite cases, as they were ejected from the gun's breech blocks. Up my nose and into my eyes went the spent cordite fumes.

After the third or fourth broadside, I most definitely failed to do my duty. What had been building up inside me for the previous hour, now erupted like Mount Etna. I was violently seasick all over my dials, the hand wheels and myself. My eyes streamed with water. I felt wretched and I smelled like the bilge of a Nova Scotia whaleboat. If someone had offered me a euthanasia pill just then, I would have taken it gladly.

After several more broadsides, "Check, Check, Check," resounded the distant voice from the TS. The starshell were bursting too low, much too low. The shoot continued without me.

"Load with armour piercing," droned the voice.

"Oh My God, help me!" I said to myself.

Crash! Bang! Bijong! Went the guns next to my head.

"Convicted murderers don't have to put up with this!" I shouted to myself over the din. Then, as suddenly as it had started, all went quiet, or had I gone deaf?

No, I eventually heard the voice of the Captain-of-the-Gun over the top of my headphones ordering, "Gun's crew, sponge out and stand down," or words to that effect.

Then I felt the turret turn and stop. I sat for what seemed ages, with only my misery and the stench as my companions. I had no way of knowing if the turret was actually locked fore and aft. I just waited and waited, smelling putrid. Eventually, everything around me went silent and so, with much trepidation, I launched myself downwards and out, into the brightly lit gun bay below. By this time, the hands were cleaning for dinner. Needless to say, before being allowed to tend to myself, I had to climb back inside the turret, armed with a bucket and scrubber, and thoroughly clean up the mess I had left behind. I missed my dinner into the bargain, which was no great loss, considering the way I was feeling.

During the afternoon, while returning to Portland, I was told to report to the Gunnery Officer in the TS. As I stood stiffly to attention before him, he told me, in very similar terms to those used by my old works foreman in Birmingham, that I would have been far better suited to joining the circus than the Navy and furthermore, that I should do my very best not to cross him over the coming two years in HMS *Solebay*. I was never again seasick. Neither, thankfully, did I have cause to cross the Gunnery Officer again. But I did, at least, understand what the Leading Cook in my new ship was up against.

Over the course of the following days and weeks, I got to know more about the ship and my new 'oppos'. As I got into the swing of things, I also dropped the small matter of how it was that I had become the 'Cook's Mate'. I was actually beginning to enjoy it. It was wintertime and while my shipmates were out on the upper decks, chipping and painting in the cold, I was learning my new trade in the warmth of the galley.

Talking with 'Dolly' one day, I was given to understand, that the ship was under the operational control of, or attached to, the Joint Services Amphibious Warfare Section, (JSAWC), whatever that may have been. At that time, it was of little concern to me personally, or to my knowledge, to any of the junior rates in the ship, whose control we were under, so long as they, whoever they were, informed us well in advance about what they intended to do with us. We sailors led fairly uncomplicated lives in those days.

I also learned that HMS *Rampart* had been constructed in 1945 and intended for service in the Far East. Before completion however, the war in that theatre came to an end and she was placed in reserve. Previously known only as L4037, she was renamed *Rampart* and re-commissioned in the mid-fifties. The ship, or *craft* as she should be known, was approximately 240ft in length, 48ft in breadth, of shallow draught, and powered by diesel engines. At the front were bow doors and a ramp, very similar to those used on modern car ferries. At the stern, was a large kedge anchor that could be used to help pull her off the beach, if necessary. An open tank deck, measuring approximately 160ft by 36ft, could be temporarily covered, using horizontal spreaders and tarpaulins. Looking forward, on either side of the tank deck, were two walkways about 6ft wide, providing access forward. Situated beneath these and with access to them through hatches in the deck, were the fridge, freezer, dry foods store, electrician's workshop, engineer's workshop and the bosun's store. That was just about it. Oh! Except to say that, for us, the 'there is also, of course, the Gunnery Branch' ratings to play on, there was just one ancient 20 millimetre Oerlikon cannon. It was neither noisy nor complicated.

The ship's complement fluctuated around the 28 eight mark most of the time. It included three officers, three non-commissioned officers and 21 junior ratings. The Commanding Officer, a Lieutenant Commander, was a real gentleman, quiet and thoughtful in character and in no way given to sudden outbursts of emotion. The First Lieutenant, the *Jimmy*, was very unlike any other First Lieutenant I had known up to that time. He did not throw his weight around and passed all his instructions to us seamen through either Scouse or the Swain, as appropriate.

The third officer, a young sub-lieutenant, acted as navigator and was known simply as *The Navvi*. The Chief Engine Room Artificer was the senior NCO in the ship and in charge of all things relating to machinery, electrical or mechanical. The Petty

Officer Coxswain was the ship's policeman and regulator. The Petty Officer Stoker was senior NCO in charge of the eight stokers in the ship. Scouse, the Leading Seaman, (I never knew his full name) was the senior seaman and known as *The Buffer*.

Of the crew, besides Scouse, several characters stood out from the rest. The Navvi was one of them. Whenever he got bored with the company of his two fellow officers, he would invariably come down to the junior ratings mess with his guitar, which he played beautifully and with which he entertained us. We quickly discovered a wash-board player and tea-chest bass player of our own and so used to have great sing-alongs. He often brought with him a half bottle of whisky. The whisky, which was strictly against the rules, was welcomed none the less by us, restricted as we were to two cans of beer each evening when at sea. Besides being the Navigator, he appeared to be pretty much everything else as well. His responsibilities included Captain's secretary, naval stores, pay, victualing, wardroom accounts, and non-seamen divisional officer.

Of those in the Junior Ratings Mess, Able Seaman Yorky Halliday was a garrulous, two-badge seaman from Dewsbury. He, together with his great oppo, Able Seaman 'Mad Jock' McConachy, from Glasgow, were larger than life characters who never seemed to be out of each other's company. Neither were they absent for lengthy periods, from standing to attention before the Captain's Table as *defaulters*. They, either individually or collectively, exhibited a strong predisposition to courting trouble. Both fine seamen and good messmates, neither of them shirked responsibility. Their presence and weight would always be felt when others were in a tight corner, whether aboard ship or ashore but both of them were always on or about the fringes of bother and were the bane of our Swains' life. The Royal Navy would never be the service it is without such men.

'Dolly' Gray, the Leading Cook, Able Seamen 'Ginger' Cartwright from Bristol, Billie Addison from the East end of London and 'Geordie' Cummings from Hartlepool were the other characters who featured prominently in matters affecting my domain on board the ship. Billie and 'Ginger' were phlegmatic characters, each having a dry sense of humour. 'Geordie', on the other hand was, well, just loud. He also demonstrated his ability to dance all of the steps of the 'Cornish Wallet Dance' when it came to contributing towards rounds of drinks. The Leading Stoker 'Pony' Moore was, with Scouse at the forefront of decisions affecting our mess. Junior by only a couple of years to Scouse, he was in charge of the mess in Scouse's absence.

The Swain was a forty-odd, testy and bilious character, who clearly did not want to be at sea during his last year in the Navy and did not brook any nonsense from those subordinate to him. We all suspected that he had a good little business going with the victuallers ashore but were never able to substantiate those suspicions. When he left us, his time in the Navy expired, he had a brand new Morris Minor 1000 delivered to the ship. 'Hmmm!' we all thought, "how could he afford such a thing on his wages?

It was good to be back in the midst of such fellows, tied together by a common cause, however important or unimportant that cause may have been. Although a very small ship, *Rampart's* daily routine, pretty much mirrored that of larger ships in the service. 'Call the Hands' was at 0645 daily except, it seems, on the day that I joined but much of the crew had been away on that singular occasion. 'Both Watches of the Hands' mustered at 0745, though instead of mustering on deck, as was normal practice in larger ships, Scouse usually detailed the seamen off for their daily work and maintenance tasks over breakfast. The stokers generally gathered by the engineers' store for the same purpose, the PO stoker being responsible for their daily routine. Evening rounds were conducted daily by the Jimmy, who dropped in at 1930 for a chat, to ensure that the mess was clean and tidy and that ratings had changed into the correct dress of the day.

The tradition of 'Saturday morning rounds' was strictly observed. Between 0800 and 1100, all hands turned to with a will, to 'clean ship'. Everything was ousted and meticulously cleaned.

Access to heads, bathroom and mess deck was severely limited. Everywhere was scrubbed and polished until whiter than white and shinier than shine. At 1100 the Swain would lead the procession, comprising the Captain and the Jimmy, on the tour of inspection. Those with responsibility for cleaning designated areas reported them ready for inspection when their turn arrived. Anything found wanting was noted and had to be corrected immediately. Items requiring repair or maintenance were logged by the Swain in the maintenance log.

Approximately one Sunday in four, *Full Divisions* was held. The ship's company, dressed in best Number 1 uniform and medals, either climbed down the vertical steel ladders into the tank deck or mustered ashore and paraded for inspection and prayers on the jetty. Inspections were very strange phenomena. There were those people, like me, who always put massive effort into ensuring that everything was just right, creases sharp and in exactly the right places, shoes gleaming, caps scrubbed, white-fronts crisply laundered and bows tied in exactly the right places. Then there were others, like Yorky and Jock for example, who just took their uniforms out of their lockers, shook them out, gave them a cursory press with a warm iron, popped them on and rubbed their shoes up the back of their legs to give them a shine. Yet, come to Divisions and Inspection, I was always one of those pulled up. The Captain would look me up and down slowly, turn to the Swain, mumble something to him and then continue on to the next in line. The Swain would bellow, "Able Seaman Barr... one step forward, march!" his voice reverberating around the little tank deck. I would quickly learn the significance of the mumble, then afterwards have to report to him with the deficiency rectified. It did not matter how much effort I put in to it, I could never look smart enough. Somehow, I always looked untidy. I even followed the Halliday-McConachy school of thought one Sunday morning and ended up standing alone in the tank deck, for an hour after hands had fallen out from divisions, as punishment for "an unusually well below par performance," as the Swain put it to me. I used to think that I was used as a marker, falling in on the end of the first row, as I did. A bit like skating or gymnastics, for example, where the first performer sets the standard and the remainder are marked either above or below that marker. On that particular occasion, I was picked up for having no creases in my bellbottom trousers. It is strange to relate now, how few people knew why sailors pressed either five or seven creases horizontally across the legs of their bellbottoms. The reason was simple. Locker space was always at such a premium in ships, large and small alike, that clothes could never be hung. They were, instead, folded neatly and tightly and packed into a steel locker, approximately two feet six inches square. Trousers were folded concertina style at the creases, and stowed so that they would remain that way, ready for the next occasion upon which they were to be worn.

The Junior Ratings mess in *Rampart* boasted one electric iron between us and our washing machines were buckets, knuckles and *dhobi dust* (soap powder). When the hands were called in the morning, it was the tradition for one of the morning watchmen to wet the tea and place it on the mess table, as the sleepy eyed incumbents jumped from their hammocks. It was no different in *Rampart*, except that we slept in bunks. On the first occasion that it fell to me to perform this task in *Rampart*, I recalled with a wry smile, one particular occasion on which I had performed the task, two or more years earlier in my first ship, HMS *Solebay*. In her, the lower deck slept in hammocks, twenty-eight to a mess. Hammocks were slung from steel bars high above the mess tables and benches. They were not permitted to be slung before nine in the evening and had to be lashed up and stowed away by thirty minutes after 'call the hands' in the morning. Men could still sit at the tables or pass along beneath them when they were slung, but only by bending almost double.

One of the older hands in the mess at that time was a three badge Able Seaman called, 'Bring 'em Back Alive Bennett', on account of the fact that he had left the Navy after twelve years, gone to Canada and enrolled for three years in the Mounted

Police. He then returned and re-joined the Navy for a further nine years. I was allocated as his 'Winger' and he was, to me, my 'Sea Daddy', I being a very junior seaman at the time. His task was to show me the ropes and generally make sure that I learned my trade. He was a scruffy, grumpy old sod, whose teeth looked like a row of soggy dog-ends in an ashtray.

Before lights out in the evening, when he retired to his hammock, he used to wedge his pipe, tobacco and false teeth between the ventilation shaft and the deck head above his hammock, ready for a light up first thing the next morning. When the hands were called, he would simply raise his hand above him, feel along the ventilator shaft for first, his teeth, then his pipe, followed by his tobacco and matches, after which a plume of smoke would be seen drifting upwards, followed by a sigh of satisfaction.

On the first occasion that I had the morning watch in the ship, I clattered down the iron ladder to the mess, with an enormous fanny of tea, which I placed on one of the mess tables. Inside the neck of the fanny was a large tea strainer, about eight inches across. I had just turned to get the mugs out of the rack, when I heard, 'Plop!' I looked back at the fanny and bending closer, I saw Bennett's false teeth lying in the strainer just below the surface of the tea. Before I had a chance to look upwards, a grizzly hand reached down from above and grasped me tightly around the neck, almost choking the life out of me. It was Bennett.

"Breathe a word to anyone 'Winger', and I'll heave you off the back of the ship in the night. Now pass my teeth up to me," he hissed.

Shaking like a leaf, I dug them out of the strainer with a fork, handed them to him and busied myself lining up the rest of the mugs ready for pouring. Meanwhile, others in the mess began to drop down onto the tabletops or benches and to lash up their hammocks. Once I had completed laying out the mugs, I fled the mess, back to my watch-keeping station underneath the sea boat. I breathed not a word about it to anyone while in the ship but many times afterwards, looking out of the corner of my eye at Bennett, I caught sight of him eyeing me up contemptuously. Neither did I, ever again, drink tea first thing in the morning in *Solebay*. I wet the tea again often enough but I never placed it anywhere near Bring 'em back alive Bennett's hammock.

Not long after joining *Rampart*, I found a billet in the Junior Ratings' Mess and so moved out of my berth in the empty Troops' Mess. There, I got to know my oppos more intimately. I say 'intimately' because, as with all small ships or submarines, living and working space was at a premium. The Junior Ratings Mess measured approximately twenty feet by thirty. Within these confines, there ate, slept, argued and played, twenty-one souls. Bunks were distributed two-high around the perimeter of the compartment. The bottom one formed seating and the upper one, when lowered, provided the backrest. There were two long Formica-topped tables and four benches. These were also used for sleeping on. Aluminium lockers were stacked three-high along one end and there were also a number of them underneath the benches. Bedding was lashed up and stowed away in the hammock netting during the daytime. The junior ratings bathroom was roughly eight feet square. It contained four aluminium washbasins, two shower cubicles and a trestle bench. The bench was used to stand your bucket on to do your *dhobying* (washing). As on all ships, its users all required the bathroom at pretty much the same times each day – first thing each morning, then again after clearing up decks in the evening.

Because a ship could only distil so much fresh water with which to replenish her fresh water supply, great care and attention was taken to limit the amount of water used. It was standard practice, in those days, to double up when using the showers. One of us climbed into the shower and 'soaked up', then stepped outside it to 'soap up', meanwhile your oppo, jumped inside and soaked up. We then swapped places again to 'rinse off' and so on. Our three-badge Leading Stoker, 'Pony' Moore, insisted on smoking his pipe throughout the showering process. When he had to stand under the water, he simply turned his pipe upside down. Upon exiting, he would re-right his pipe and carry on puffing as before. The dirty old sod. We used to give him a real hard time over it but he could not be deterred. He just used to reply, "If you can't take it shipmates, then you shouldn't have joined." It was just routine for him. Jumping into the shower after him one day, Scouse burned the sole of his foot on the fallen contents of the Leading Stokers' pipe. The bathroom was full of bodies at that precise moment. First of all there was silence, then a screech from Scouse, after which, mayhem broke loose. Dhobi buckets were sent flying in all directions as 'Pony' Moore's feet grappled for traction. When eventually they gripped, he flew out of the bathroom door and onto the port side walkway with Scouse close on his heels, threatening to throw him overboard when he caught hold of him. The flight led up to the foredeck. There followed a standoff between the pair of them, until both turned blue with cold and they had to retreat, back to the warmth and shelter of the bathroom, Scouse limping horribly, while 'Pony' kept a healthy distance behind him. He was banned from smoking in the bathroom after that. It was all the more grotesque because they were both close on being the oldest members of the ship's company and neither of them cut a pretty sight on the upper deck in their white nakedness. Incidentally, the term 'old' to me at that time meant anyone over the age of thirty-five!

Just prior to Christmas, we slipped our berth alongside *Vanguard* and returned to the coaling jetty, to keep HMS *Plover* company. I never really found out why we had been tethered to *Vanguard* in the first place. We were unlikely companions. Unbeknown to us, *Vanguard* was making final preparations for towing to the breaker's yard. Had I known that beforehand, I would have explored her more thoroughly, as she was the last of a class dating back to the Dreadnoughts.

Christmas leave came and I, together with eight others, vol-unteered to take second, or 'retard' leave, as it was called. The main leave party took Christmas and the New Year, while we, the retard leave party, took the first two weeks in January. When the main leave party returned after their leave, looking disconsolate, we gave them the usual barracking, 'Second leave is best', a term that resonates amongst matelots and is always the tongue-in-cheek taunt of the retard leave party, for whom life has been reasonably quiet and relaxed while the main leave party was away. However, while the retard leave party go off on their holidays they know full well that the returning main leave party will be digging out, preparing the ship for sea again.

'Calling the Hands' in the mornings was the daily task of the duty quartermaster. Many 'ditties' were used over ships' Tannoy systems to rouse their crews out of their hammocks or bunks. The task fell to me on many occasions. The best that I could muster was:

> *Wakey, Wakey, Wakey,*
> *Rise and shine the morning's fine*
> *Heave ho, heave ho, heave ho, lash up and stow*
> *Curb your dreams and comb your locks*
> *Hands off cocks, on socks.*

A far better effort was heard one day over the Tannoy of the cruiser HMS *Blake*, the morning after their main leave party had returned:

> *Time to get up today is the day*
> *Second leavers are going away*
> *Stow your gear into your grip*
> *Time to leave this mighty ship*
> *First leavers returning, don't they look sad?*
> *Well hard luck lads, it's not so bad*
> *You've had your leave, don't look so down*
> *Tonight it's our turn on the town*
> *Drinking beer and chasing lasses*
> *Heaving up and breaking glasses*
> *When I come back, you all may scoff*
> *But you can't crack me 'cause I'm just off*
> *And so I say to all the rest*
> *Don't forget... second leave's best!*

We, the retard leave party, had a very pleasant but quiet Christmas. With 'Dolly' Gray having to take main leave, I cooked for those remaining aboard. I cooked the Christmas dinner as best I could, given that I had only had six weeks in the job. I worked fastidiously, remembering everything that I had recently been taught. In the event, there were no complaints. We had roast turkey and stuffing, roast potatoes and two veg, besides which, the 'Swain' had bought us a pre-cooked pudding. I was, however, glad to see the main leave party return and to take my turn. This was only the second or third time that I had been home since disembarkation leave from HMS *Solebay* in May. My mother, father and sister were pleased to see me, as was my girlfriend Jackie. What she saw in the long distance relationship that we then had, I do not know. I had met her a week before sailing for the Far East nearly two years earlier and we had written to each other pretty well monthly ever since.

One day during my leave, while passing Grice's shop on my way into town, I peeped furtively through the open doorway, more out of curiosity than a real desire to encounter their daughter again, although there was no doubting that I was feeling a whole lot more confident in my abilities to mingle with the opposite sex these days. But she was nowhere to be seen. Later, my sister Andrene told me that Grice's daughter had gone off to university or college. I never saw her again.

Before returning from leave, I bought a car, a 1946 MGTC. I exchanged one hundred and twenty seven pounds for it; all the money I had saved since joining up. I only bought it in the first place because my girlfriend had kept saying to me that she fancied going out with a bloke who owned a Jaguar. This had begun to irk me somewhat. There was fat chance of that on my wages, so I bought the MG instead, hoping that would impress her enough keep her interested. When I told her what I had bought, she turned her nose up. Once having been for a spin in it with the hood down though, she gave it seven out of ten, so I felt on much safer ground after that.

However, I still had to pass my driving test. I had booked this as soon as I had been informed of my leave dates. Dressed in my Number 1 suit, I arrived at the test centre on the appointed day and commenced my driving test, hoping that my uniform would sway any fifty-fifty decisions my way. I had the soft-top of the car rolled down, to create, I hoped, an impression of 'total confidence'. Unfortunately, in my intoxication with 'total confidence', I had omitted to note that it was January and that the light drizzle falling had turned to rain. I observed, immediately, that the examiner was not too happy climbing into the damp bucket seat of an open sports car, even if I was. He seemed even less impressed, when, having suggested to me that we could not continue unless I could get the hood up, I could not. Well, I did eventually, after a long struggle, never having done it before. The hood, when secured up, turned out to be great for the examiners protection, no doubt about that, but for my driving visibility it was turgid. The rain droplets on the flimsy celluloid side and back screens, pretty well prevented me from seeing anything at all. Upon my reversing around a nearside corner, I ran down a parked bicycle, then, whilst parking between two vehicles, I allegedly ran over a drunken bystander's foot. He was trying his hardest to guide me into the space, not realising that I was undertaking my driving test. He did not help matters much by dancing around in pain right in front of the examiner. How thoughtless of him!

But the smell of his breath and his bleary eyes probably saved me. Just then, the sleety rain turned to snow. Believing that I had blown my test, I drove the rest of it in my usual, belligerent mood, finally skidding to a halt outside the test centre on completion. I mentally dared the examiner to find fault in my driving. To my utter astonishment, he gave me a pass! He based this, he said, firstly upon my ability to react effectively to differing driving conditions and secondly, for making him feel safe in difficult circumstances. He did add a caveat, though, that I really should get to know how my car functioned a little better, before inviting others into it. I thanked him kindly and was inwardly elated.

Upon returning from leave, the ship underwent several weeks of maintenance, painting, greasing and so on. When painting-ship, it is usual practice to close off any heads and bathrooms whose outlet pipes are in the close vicinity to the side of the ship being painted, thus ensuring that neither the painted areas nor the painters are fouled. One day, just as we were completing painting, Ginger had a rather unfortunate accident due to someone having forgotten to rope off the junior ratings' heads. Ginger was sat alone on a *stage* (plank of wood) suspended from the guardrail, just above the water line but below the outlet pipe from the heads. As he was painting away merrily, someone used the heads, then flushed away the previous night's *Bengal Trouser Fouler* (curry).

Yells and curses from below brought those of us who heard them rushing to the rail, where we witnessed Ginger, still sitting on the wooden stage below, his head and shoulders festooned with toilet paper and second-hand curry. That we all fell about laughing did not make him any the happier and he threatened there and then to skewer the man responsible for failing to lock off the heads. We all gave Ginger a wide berth for the rest of that day. The following morning at breakfast he was still grumbling on about people not doing their jobs properly and not showing sufficient reverence to older hands like himself. It was at this point that 'Mad Jock' McConachy turned to him and said, "Ginger! I left the poxy heads unlocked. Now either shut up about it or follow me down to the bosun's store, where we'll sort it out between us."

That brought an abrupt end to Ginger's grumbling!

The Captain informed us one Sunday morning that we were to proceed to Poole in Dorset, to embark some small craft or other. On completion, we were to sail to Westward Ho, on the coast of North Devon. This news was welcomed by all aboard. It also created quite a buzz amongst those who had been there earlier the previous year.

One cold but bright morning in March, 'Special Sea Du-tymen' were called to their stations, all water tight doors and hatchways were closed and we stood by to leave Portsmouth. We singled up mooring lines and slipped for sea, saying farewell to what had become our 'buddy' ship, *Plover*. Departing Portsmouth Dockyard, we left to port, the mighty *Vanguard* and Flagstaff Steps, home of the Flag Officer and, to starboard, the Reserve Fleet and the old *Foudroyant*. We proceeded out past the breakwater and into the Solent. By the time we reached the Nab tower, the unfortunate 'Dolly' was writing down instructions on his chalkboard, should he be struck down with seasickness.

He was in the middle of preparing a shepherds' pie as we passed the Needles when, quite expectedly, he turned suddenly to me and said, "Over to you *Skin* (a young sailor not possessed of a five o'clock shadow), you know what's required... and don't forget the gravy." He did not surface again until we were well inside Poole Harbour that evening.

At the time he left the galley for his bunk, there was a long swell rolling up the Channel from the west and our bluff bows thumped right into it. I quickly secured the restraining bars on the range, to prevent the various pots moving around, placed all things moveable into drawers and cupboards and completed the preparations that he had so suddenly been forced to abandon. 'Hands to Dinner' was called at midday and I had the *scran* (food) completed by 11:45. There was always a 15-minute leeway in any case, due to *Tot Time*. 'Up Spirits' was piped at 11:55 each day. This tradition, going back to Nelson's day, was still rigidly observed in Her Majesty's ships around the world. Those sailors over the age of twenty, who so desired, were permitted to *draw their tot*. The tot, comprising one part rum to two parts water, was issued under the eagle eye of the Officer of the Day in harbour or the Supply Officer at sea. Rum was measured from the barrel into the *Rum Fanny* of each mess. The correct amount of water was then added, after which the mess *Rum Bosun* returned with the fanny to the mess. Then, using the correct measure, it was ceremoniously doled out in glasses to those entitled to it. Senior Rates were allowed to take their tot neat.

Rum was a currency, considered by all in the Navy to have superior bargaining power to money. Debts owed to shipmates for favours granted or services rendered were called in daily on the mess decks of all HM ships. Small favours were paid for in *sippers* (one finger's width from the top of the glass), greater favours with *gulpers* (two fingers width from the top) and major favours – for example catching hold of your oppo's oilskin and preventing him from being washed overboard – could be worth *half a tot* or even *a full tot*, depending upon the value your oppo placed on his life. Money never changed hands in those days. All of us who witnessed the passing of The Tot into history in 1967 observed a major change in many sailors' proclivity towards the service; let nobody tell you otherwise. When they took away the Tot, they took away the pre-eminent stimulus for promoting a sense of community within ships. Sailors lived in individual messes, their homes within the ship, according to their branch or trade. They had no reason to enter others messes unless invited but at Tot Time aboard any ship of the fleet, as many as a third of the crew could be found in messes other than their own, sharing a tot and a yarn with people they may not have seen for days, weeks or even months. I have been in stokers and bunting tossers' messes, conversing with guys who I would not otherwise have met during the course of a commission, and likewise, invited many of them into my own mess at Tot Time. So when the Tot went, with it went much of the community spirit. The stimulus was removed and, overnight, the comings and goings of sailors between messes ceased.

Arriving in Poole just before sunset, we berthed starboard side to, alongside the main harbour wall. Being used, as I was, to laying alongside in great Naval Dockyards, this was a real treat. It was like being next to the main road. It was also very handy because, just across the way, stood the Jolly Sailor Inn. In no time at all the ship was secured and all but the Officer of the

Day, the Duty Quartermaster and the Duty Stoker took their leave and established themselves in the public bar. From the 'Hello Maisy' and 'Alright Pony?' it was clear that many of Rampart's crew were re-acquainting themselves with old friends here. Indeed, the ship frequented the port regularly, there being a 'JSAWC' camp close by.

Our period of stay in Poole spanned a weekend, so some of us took leave and the train, up to the *Big Smoke* (London). The leading cook had recovered now that we were in harbour, which released me for the weekend. Upon my return on the Monday morning, I was flabbergasted to see the tank deck full of brightly coloured sailing yachts. Settling into the mess, I remarked casually, to no one in particular, "What on earth have we got here then chaps, the 'Yellow Wellie Brigade?'"

"The Skipper's on the make," grumbled someone.

Well, it did seem a rather peculiar cargo for a 'tank landing craft'. We slipped our berth later that afternoon. Westward Ho! via Plymouth, was our destination but not before a dozen or so of the yacht crews left the Jolly Sailor Inn and came aboard. They managed to keep out of the way of the preparations being made to leave harbour but, perched as they were along the starboard rail, they made the ship look untidy and unseaman-like. They kept themselves pretty well to themselves, sleeping overnight and eating their own rations on their yachts. Next morning, we entered Plymouth Sound, where we disembarked them onto Mountbatten slipway. As the operation was taking place, the Swain tried in vain to explain to us that they were all boats belonging to the RNSA (Royal Naval Sailing Association), used for both recreation and instructional purposes. He went on to say that any of us could join the RNSA if we wished to learn to sail and that these boats were currently being returned to their base at Plymouth. This explanation did not satisfy the more sceptical amongst us, in particular the *Janners* (Devonport based ratings) on board, as no sooner were the bow doors secured than we stood out of Plymouth Sound and away to the southwest, without giving them leave.

"That bloody well proves what I was saying," grumbled one of them. "The Skipper is definitely on the make. They were civvies, they were. Did you not see the length of some of their hair?"

"Stop *manking* (complaining) you bleeding Janner," chorused the rest of us. We had little sympathy for them, even though we knew that one or two had wives and families there, just a stone's throw away. But what the hell, they were only Janners after all, weren't they? "Up Pompey!"

We continued on down the Channel and through the gap between Land's End and the Scilly Isles. There was quite a large swell abroad and we, being flat-bottomed, rolled about like a drunken sailor. Dolly kept his own counsel, alone in his cot in the troops mess deck, until we were well up into the Bristol Channel. Two days after leaving Poole and with 'Dolly' back at his place in the galley again, we pitched into Barnstaple Bay on the incoming tide, crossed the bar and veered up the Torridge Estuary. We left Westward Ho! and Appledore to starboard, the river Taw and Instow to port and berthed port side to against Zeta Berth, a small, floating pontoon moored to the riverbank, midway between Instow and Bideford-East-the-Water. It was my first ever visit to this part of the world but it was an area with which I was to become extremely familiar and to work in, in a civilian capacity, many years later. At that moment, though, it was a strange feeling, looking shoreward from the short gangway, seeing only trees and fields beyond the little pontoon but it was the kind of sight I became accustomed to in my time with *Rampart*. I had hitherto been used to seeing dockyard cranes and bustling jetties when looking shoreward. Here, I could hear cars passing just the other side of the trees but could not see a road from our low-lying position.

Within a few minutes of securing alongside, those of us whose first visit it was to this berth were surprised to hear a train whistle close at hand. Moments later, we were astonished to see a tank engine and two coaches clatter by, just yards from the end of the short pontoon, between it and the road beyond. You could have reached out an arm and touched it. Once past us, it slowed down as it rounded the bend and clanked to a halt in a cloud of steam at Instow station, less than a quarter of a mile away. We matelots, travelled on that train on many occasions, to and from either Barnstaple or Bideford. The line, sadly, is no more, having been axed in the Beeching cuts in the mid-sixties.

It was one of those wonderful little West Country estuary branch lines, similar to those that connected Wadebridge with Padstow and Axmouth with Axminster. The line, coming in from Halwill Junction, followed the river Torridge from just North West of the town of Torrington, through Bideford, Instow and Fremmington to Barnstaple. As the train rattled along, so the view from its carriage windows changed, perceptively. Between Torrington and Bideford, one looked out upon the fast flowing river Torridge and the green fields beyond it. As the landscape flattened out, the character of the river changed. It widened and became tidal, as it wound its way aimlessly down towards Bideford and the Bristol Channel. Beyond Bideford itself, the estuary opened out, permitting boats and small ships to navigate up to the town quay. Small craft of every description could be seen, some moored up on the gently sloping banks and others plying their trade along the river itself. Then, onwards the train rocked, down past our berth to Instow, where in the summer holidaymakers thronged the sandy beachfront. It was a favourite spot for fishermen, many of whom could be seen, sat hunched over their rods along the water's edge, staring out across the water to Appledore, whose whitewashed houses tumbled, higgledy-piggledy, down to the water's edge. After a short stop at Instow, the train rattled and swayed through the sand dunes to Fremington and beyond to Barnstaple and the river Taw. You changed trains in Barnstaple for Exeter.

The Janners got their own back on us here, as they were just a couple of hours from home by rail, whereas, for the remainder of us, the journey time home was far too great for a long or short weekend. Therefore, on the first Saturday lunchtime, off to Plymouth the three Janners went.

This was a lovely part of the world to visit. The old pubs in Instow and in Appledore were charming, while the people in them were full of character. That first Sunday, Divisions were held on the small pontoon. To our surprise, a crowd of onlookers, who presumably had come to see what this strange craft was that had come amongst them, were treated to the spectacle. I was picked up again, for having bent my hat too far down at the sides, giving it a far too 'rakish' look. Once bent, it could not be properly straightened, so I was told to replace it the next time we were in Portsmouth. Jock's hat was in far worse condition than mine but, as usual, his didn't warrant a second glance.

The road upon which we could hear traffic was just the other side of the rail bed but lower than the embankment. We walked this road into Instow to catch the bus or train when wanting to go further afield than Instow itself. When the tide receded, the ship was left high and dry on the sand. On Saturday afternoons and Sundays, when the tide was out, we played football on the hard sand, using the open bow doors for the goal. Tide permitting, you could, if you were brave and did not mind getting wet up to the knees, save the train fare, by wading across the river to Appledore and the pubs there. Mostly, however, we wanted to visit the larger town of Barnstaple. It was considered likely that there would be a greater selection of pretty maidens there, ready to be swept off their feet at the sight of a few Jolly Jack Tars. As things turned out, that was not the case. It never was, except in the minds of us dreamers. The first onshore party of us liberty men to visit that fair town got into a spot of bother in a pub there on our first night ashore. Eight or nine of us climbed into our best number one suits before proceeding ashore at around seven thirty, when we walked the half mile into Instow. There we caught the train to Barnstaple. Mad Jock and Yorky Halliday were amongst those who had been here before and so knew the pubs well.

"There is always loads of fanny in the White Hart," enthused Jock, as we left Barnstaple station on foot, walking the few hundred yards to the pub, situated just off the Strand. There, we ordered up our first round. After a fairly frosty reception, during which light-hearted insults were thrown between ourselves and a group of local lads at the other end of the bar, things lightened up for about an hour or so but, it seemed, there remained an uneasy peace.

We sat in a group in a corner by the window, where we pretty well got on with the job in hand, of drinking ourselves stupid. We had no other agenda that first night in town. They, the local lads, amused themselves at the other end of the bar playing darts, no problem there. However, the touch-paper was not that far away, though no-one knew what it looked like just then. It finally materialised in the shape of several young lovelies, jiving in front of the juke box. Yorky and Jock, sooner than anyone expected, put a match to the touch-paper by moving in and taking up with two of them. Glancing around at the faces at the other end of the bar, it soon became clear to the rest of us that the local lads were not about to be pushed passively to one side whilst a few visiting matelots, starved of female company, got amongst their womenfolk. Whether or not they were interested in them themselves, did not seem to matter. The natives, as they say, were becoming restless. The previously nondescript glances thrown in our direction now became sullen stares and the mutterings between them became almost audible. The game of darts was put to one side.

Yorky and Jock remained oblivious to the rapidly deteriorating situation until the unexpected arrival by air of a barstool. Fortunately for the dancers, it connected only with the juke box before clattering noisily to the floor. That hitherto inoffensive piece of furniture, now lying awkwardly against the foot of the jukebox, would be a lethal weapon in the hands of either Mad Jock McConachy or Yorky Halliday unless they could be contained and the barstool removed. Before anyone could move, the pub erupted and, amid wild shouts and screams, the occupants of the pub suddenly and as one were sucked into the vortex in the middle of the floor.

Both sides struggled manfully, either to contain their own or to get at the opposition. The independents just tried to get between the protagonists, like a referee trying to separate two boxers in a clinch. The three of us nearest to Mad Jock immediately fell upon him in an attempt to restrain him. By now, he had the barstool in one hand and what smelt like a farmhand in the other. We were of one mind, to wrestle him away and out of the front door as quickly as we could. That was no easy matter, however, as he was well over six feet and weighed fifteen or so stones. Yorky, on the other hand, who was similar in stature and with four others desperately trying to drag him back, led the charge in the opposite direction. Eventually, we broke Jock's hold on his adversary and pulled him outside, away from the throng. All four of us were huffing and puffing from the effort. We could not leave him there and return to the fray because he would have been back inside in the blink of an eyelid. Trusting the others to follow, Geordie and I dragged, pushed and shoved Mad Jock to a taxi rank on the Strand and into a waiting taxi. The other two went back to assist Yorky. I was bleeding from a cut lip, caused by Jock's elbow, while Geordie had a badly swollen cheekbone. We arrived back at the ship 45 minutes later and two pounds poorer, with Mad Jock still threatening to kill anyone who laid a finger on any of his shipmates. *That's rich*, I thought, *him having thumped at least two of us already*. The others returned to the ship a good hour or so after us, with the barstool as a trophy. Some of them also sported cuts and bruises to remember the night by, although strangely none of the injuries had been caused by the opposition. Most of all we suffered from injured pride.

In the inevitable wash up that followed, it was discovered that Yorky had offered to settle the matter outside the pub with any one of those who chose to take him on. A suitable candidate was being pushed forward to meet his challenge when, before an honourable outcome could be concluded, the local constabulary arrived. As there had been no fighting, there had been no public order offence committed and so no arrests were made. The police contented themselves with seeing the two factions on their way in opposite directions.

It also came to light, the day after, that trouble had occurred in that particular pub on previous occasions that the ship's company had visited. Barnstaple was then put out of bounds to us for the remainder of our stay, so an honourable settlement was never achieved and pride was never restored.

'That's very unfair', we thought, but seemingly inevitable. I would not have put it past Jock and Yorky to have announced in advance our intentions that night, such was their propensity for fun and games. Jock, railed against those of us who had restrained him, for making him desert his oppo in the midst of danger. Weeks later we were still saying to him, "Put a sock in it Jock, for Christ's sake!" Even Yorky agreed with us, promising Jock that he would arrange another opportunity for him to come to his aid on some future occasion. We had to content ourselves with the rather more agricultural bars of Bideford and Instow for the remainder of our stay.

Barnstaple Bay is at the confluence of two important rivers, the Torridge and the Taw. Over the centuries, silt from these rivers has created a wide, gently-sloping sandy bay, forming a large protective sand bar at its outer limit. At the eastern end of the bay is Braunton Burrows, an area of outstanding natural beauty, covered with huge sand dunes and a favourite destination for holidaymakers and surfers. It also provided an ideal location for the trials that we were about to undertake.

On the western side of the bay lies the village of Westward Ho! with its long grey stone bank and low lying grasslands beyond it. Several days after our excursion to Barnstaple, we undertook some beach landing drills, just off Braunton Burrows. We ran in, dropping our big kedge anchor astern, about a hundred metres or so before beaching. On the final part of each run, the *strongback* was removed from the bow doors, enabling them to be winched open just as we touched ground. Next came the ramp. It went down with a splash, maybe twenty or thirty metres from dry land. Each drill was timed and lessons learned were knitted into subsequent runs. We also took part in another trial during our stay. At Fremmington there was (and remains still) a small JSAWC base. Here, one sunny morning, we took delivery of a solitary tank. It had, attached to it, an outer hull. It was designed to swim ashore under its own steam, divest itself of its protective hull when it had safely done so, then proceed to do the job that tanks do best. It was the queerest of shapes. This one was an improved version of a design that had been around since the Second World War. Accompanying it was its two-man crew and several white-coated boffins. We could tell that they were boffins by their appearance. They were, without exception, bald-headed, with just a few wisps of grey hair around the sides and back. They looked, for all the world, like brothers.

With our cargo aboard, we manoeuvred out into the bay, ready to release our solitary tank. My part in this exercise is almost unworthy of a mention, other than to say that sailors do not work well on empty stomachs. Geordie and I were sat on a couple of stools on the after deck, making a pretty poor job of peeling potatoes. He and I, being nearest to the ship's motor boat, lowered it to the water and secured it astern when ordered to do so. This was later manned by two seamen who, after cranking its ancient engine into life, motored off in a cloud of black smoke to act as safety boat.

Geordie and I had, by this time, lost interest in what was happening up for'ard. In any case, no excuses would be entertained if dinner were not ready on time. It was as peaceful as could be back aft; only the cries of hundreds of gulls, mistaking us for a trawler, disturbed the tranquillity. Geordie, becoming bored, looked at me and said, "Watch this..." He then threw a peeled potato into the air, where it was quickly set upon by three or four gulls. One managed to wrest it from the others but in doing so got the potato stuck on or in its beak and it plunged headlong into the water. Geordie was beside himself with laughter.

"You're not only tight, Geordie, but sick as well,' I told him. "Next time you go to the heads, exercise your brain and give your right hand a rest." The gull reappeared on the surface, I am pleased to say, none the worse for wear.

Presently, there came drifting aft to us, the sound of voices raised in alarm. These quickly became more urgent and pronounced. By the time we moved from our perches to where we could get a good view of what was happening, two guys were being fished out of the water and into the safety boat. Of the tank, there was no sign whatsoever. Dinner was well delayed as frantic efforts were made to locate it. Eventually, it was left to be salvaged at low water by JSAWC Base personnel. Over dinner, the story unfolded, such as there was to tell. With the boffins stood on the foc's'le, providing instructions to the driver, the vehicle slowly trundled out onto to the edge of the ramp, after which it lurched forward and into the water, like a duckling from a riverbank. It then commenced its passage towards the beach, some two hundred or so metres away, but after a minute or two was seen to ship water over its protective sides. Fortunately, the two crewmembers had the time and the acumen to bale out before it disappeared beneath the surface altogether.

"Oh well, back to the drawing board chaps," someone cracked loudly towards the boffins. They, of course, being far better educated and having greater presence of mind, ignored the flippant remark completely. Bless them. Before leaving the scene, we dropped a Dan Buoy over the side to mark the tank's last known position. By the time we departed from Barnstaple Bay, at the end of the week, the tank was safely back ashore, undergoing detailed inspection.

We left from Zeta Berth three weeks, after having had our one and only run ashore in Barnstaple. On the way back to Portsmouth, we called in at Poole Harbour, where we exercised with the Royal Marines in Studland Bay, as well as renewing our acquaintances with the patrons of The Jolly Sailor. News shortly filtered down to us via the Swain that our next destination was to be Caen and Rouen, where we were to assist in celebrating the sixteenth anniversary of the greatest invasion of all time, the D-Day Landings of June 6th 1944. There was also an unconfirmed buzz going around that, on completion of the D-Day celebrations, we were headed for the Arctic Circle and northern Norway. And so it was that we departed from Poole for Portsmouth, to begin our preparations.

The following day was my twentieth birthday, a landmark for me because I was no longer 'under-age' and now eligible to draw my tot of rum, along with the men. Also, I'd get Dolly to stop calling me *skin*. Tot time came and, in keeping with tradition, I took my tot first. Then, to mark my coming of age, I took 'sippers' from the other fifteen or so in the mess who were drawing their tots. My memory of what happened next escapes me! I remember waking up in my bunk at around four thirty or five and looking down at Scouse, who was reading a book in the bunk below me in an otherwise empty mess. He was my watch-keeper that afternoon and sat there to make sure no harm came to me. How I miss that camaraderie today! In the event, I could not face my tot for two or three days afterwards, so I had it put back into the rum fanny for *Queen's* – the dregs left in the rum fanny when everyone had drawn their tots, which was handed around to all eligible until finished.

5.   Caen, Rouen and the Unfortunate Pierre

From 'Coastwise'

Spruce and natty, spick and span,
Before the wind the schooner ran.
Fresh and dewy, neat and tidy,
Standing off for Aberidy.

    Richard Barr

The ship gave leave to each watch and once again I managed to wangle retard leave party, on account that Dolly Gray was going off to attend his sister's wedding. Between the main leave party returning and the retard leave party departing, the Jimmy gathered us together to inform us that, following the Norway trip, we were tasked to support the guard ship at Cowes for the duration of Cowes Week, the International Sailing Regatta, which was scheduled for the end of July. In addition, at the beginning of September we were to take part in an exercise to test the readiness of the Civil Defence Organisation to react in the event of a disaster. Never before had we been provided with so much advance warning of our future movements.

During my leave, I travelled with Billie Addison up to London for a couple of days, before continuing on home to Birmingham. I had never really discovered the capital because I normally used it solely as a staging post to get to and from home. Waterloo and Euston stations, the tube and the taxis between them, were, with one exception, my only previous experiences of the capital. Billie lived in Hackney and I stayed there with him for two days. It turned out to be a real eye-opener for me. His parents' house was still lit by gaslight and certainly smelled that way. We visited all his local haunts and I met his friends and family. I was quite envious because, although coming from a large city myself, I had moved around a lot more as a child, following my father, and therefore had never developed lasting friendships, as Billie seemed to have done. I had actually attended four secondary schools, in different towns, between the age of eleven and fifteen. Billie was one of five children and all of them but him still lived at home. I had only one schoolfriend left that I could name, whereas nearly everyone we passed in the street he hailed as an old mate from his schooldays. I was truly mesmerised by the number of old acquaintances that came up to him to enquire of his well-being and then, looking straight at me, enquired of him as to the odd company he was now keeping. I began to think that they were a funny lot as well but kept it to myself! We visited his local pub the first night in town, where he was greeted like a long-lost son the moment we walked through the door. It was quite fascinating and another world to mine entirely.

I did not understand much of the conversations that took place that weekend as Billie immediately adopted a rather more pronounced version of his native cockney dialect to that with which he normally regaled his shipmates. When among his kith and kin, he quite naturally reverted to his roots.

That Saturday evening Billie and his mates discussed the possibilities of the pair of us playing football the following day. He agreed that it would be fun, while I was less certain but after a couple more pints, he talked me round without too much difficulty, saying that he would fix me up with a pair of boots. My last stalling tactic overcome, I gave in and that was that. On Sunday morning, at around ten, we walked over to Hackney Marshes. I had never in my life before seen so many football pitches upon which so many teams wore so many different coloured shirts. I estimated that there were over a thousand footballers on the Marshes that morning.

By enquiring around to find out who was short-handed, we both managed to get a game. I was the first to be fixed up, so Billie went off towards another crowd who were preparing to start their game. I couldn't tell you who I played for or against. I only remember that I was handed a blue and yellow jersey and told to stay out of trouble on the right wing. I received a badly bruised shoulder and what I took to be a right bollocking from the rest of the team for missing the only good opportunity we had to score during the whole of the game. The funny thing was, I didn't understand a word anyone said to me, not because they spoke cockney but because none of them spoke English. I was later given to understand that I had played for a team of Greek Cypriot restaurateurs and waiters, who were playing a team comprising Maltese restaurateurs and waiters. It was a bad-tempered affair, with much gesticulating and shrugging of shoulders whenever the referee gave a decision not to the liking of the various combatants. On one particular occasion, when the referee spoke to me about a foul I had committed, when I did not shrug my shoulders or challenge his decision, he looked at me askance, as if to say 'who the hell are you and where did you learn your football?' Frankly, I was pleased when it was all over and had handed my shirt back to a surly-looking fat guy with greasy hair and a large holdall. He looked like the kind of fellow who might quietly dispose of people who missed golden opportunities, so I was keen to put some distance between us and wandered off to look for Billie.

Half an hour later I spied him, sat alone on a bench and seemingly in some considerable pain. It transpired that he had taken a bad knock to his hip but, other than that, he was chuffed that he had scored the winning goal in his game. Without more ado, I took hold of his arm, shoved it gingerly around my bruised shoulder and we hobbled off in the direction of the changing facilities. It was a half mile back to where we had changed, together with hundreds of others. On our arrival there, we found the place a teeming mass of humanity, searching for shoes, clothing, tracksuits and the like, which only two hours earlier had been thrown down in haste by their exuberant owners. It took an age to locate all my kit and I eventually left without my socks, they being nowhere to be found. Knowing so many people, Billie had no problem in cadging a lift for us both on the back of a milk float that happened to be driven by an old schoolmate of his. Back at his house, I politely refused to sit down to Sunday lunch, as I wanted to get off to Euston to catch my train, so that afternoon, a little sore, a little wiser and without socks, I was sent on my onward journey home, laden with enough corned beef and pickle sandwiches to feed our ship's company.

During my two weeks leave, I took the opportunity to go and visit Jack and Lucy near Ludlow. It was my first visit to them since leaving there six years earlier, a pimply youth of fourteen. I went in my uniform, to impress upon them that their efforts to turn me into a useful and well-behaved young man had had some effect. I also took my girlfriend Jackie with me, to add further evidence. Jack and Lucy were undoubtedly pleased to see me and put up a wonderful tea of sandwiches, homemade scones and strawberry jam, but as neither of them had ever been prone to give much praise, even where their own three children were concerned, I came away feeling somewhat deflated. It was not their fault; rather it was mine. I was looking for recognition that perhaps I did not especially deserve. They were salt-of-the-earth, down-to-basics people and to gain any adulation from them you had to have achieved something very special indeed. But at least it was an enjoyable day out. Although my mother, father and sister continued to keep in contact with them, I, sadly, saw them on just one further occasion. That day was one of just three or four during that particular leave that I spent with Jackie, as I had a lot of work to do to get my car ready for the road again. It had been left outside in the snow and rain and presented a sorry sight when I returned home. I had become tired of the long haul by rail and the uncomfortable journey by coach, so I decided to go back to Portsmouth in my own car at the end of my leave. My father helped me to give the engine a good de-coke, something he did on his own cars every six months or so. I therefore returned from Easter leave in my first car, for the first time ever. I was very proud to be the dashing young owner of a gleaming black MG. I felt by then that I had come to know enough people in or around Portsmouth, who I could ask to allow me to park my car on their premises from time to time, whilst I was away at sea.

It was a lovely spring day when finally I drove my pride and joy up to Unicorn Gate, at the entrance to Portsmouth Dockyard. Showing my identity card to the policeman, he shook his head and said, "Sorry young man, you must have a pass to bring a private car into the yard and you can only get one of those if you are able to show that you have extremely extenuating circumstances."

He put additional emphasis on the word 'extremely'. Few sailors had private cars at that time and those who did were not catered for, as later became the case.

"Oh well, where is the safest place for me to park up for a week then?' I asked.

"There is an open car park outside Marlborough Gate where a lot of the dockyard personnel park their cars," he replied, pointing towards Pitt Street.

At that very moment, two separate cars, containing officers, swept past me and through the gate with just a nod from the policeman. Feeling a little pissed off, as quite naturally you would, I backed up, turned and headed in the direction he had indicated. When I arrived there, I discovered that it was nothing more than a bombsite, half-full of wrecked cars. Under the circumstances, there was nothing else that I could do other than leave it there and try to visit it as often as my duties permitted, although I doubted that it would be in one piece the next time I saw it.

'That's just typical of me,' I thought. 'If I ever fall into a barrel of tits, I'll come up sucking my own thumb!'

During the following week, I earnestly set out to find a more permanent home for my car while in Portsmouth. I had rung an old mate from Barracks who, with his wife of just a few months, rented a house in Hilsea. He told me that he had a driveway but no car. Unfortunately for me, he was away on a course the first time I called him, so I tried him again later that week.

"That's not a problem, mate," he said, when I contacted him at length. "You can leave it here anytime you want to. I'll keep an eye on it for you. It'll cost you though!"

"OK," I said, "half a tot. Come round tomorrow." In the event, he came round for the next three days, but it was worth it to me.

With all the crew safely back from leave and my car safely parked at my mate's house, we stored ship and prepared for our next engagement. Two of our crew, a Stoker and the Leading Electrician, had left the ship during the leave period and their replacements had joined. When I returned from leave, they were already settled into the mess. We also embarked a couple of dozen Royal Marines who were to accompany us to France. It was now the beginning of June and we departed Portsmouth again, this time setting course for Normandy. All of us were feeling a little humbled to be travelling in the wake of the hundreds of thousands of others who had embarked in similar craft to ours sixteen years earlier, in the greatest seaborne invasion the world had ever known. The following afternoon we entered the river Orme and cruised leisurely up towards Caen. On the way there, we passed through Pegasus Bridge, the swing-bridge beside the pockmarked café immortalised in the epic film *The Longest Day*. There, we disembarked the Marines, who held a short service beside the old café, now a national monument. We continued on to our berth in Caen while the Royal Marines went on by road, they having other engagements to fulfil. During our stay in Caen, all but the duty watch took leave to visit the magnificent open museum at Arromanches, where the epic story of the invasion unfolds before your very eyes. To gaze upon the remains of the Mulberry Harbour, the assault beaches and the defence positions, so excellently preserved, brought lumps to many of our throats. The museum is more a diary of events as they unfolded on 6th June 1944, from the moment the first assault troops touched down. I remember seeing hundreds of tiny lights depicting different units engaging and eventually overcoming the entrenched enemy along the whole of the Normandy Coast in a scale model of the battle-field. It was a truly remarkable replay in miniature of the real event sixteen years earlier. We also visited some of the many defence bunkers that had been preserved. For anyone not understanding the full impact of the first few days of the invasion of Europe, Arromanches is a great place to go and learn.

The following day our ship was open to visitors. On larger, more technically interesting warships, 'open ship' is an event to be savoured by the public and ships' crews alike. Sailors are proud to show people around their ship and to answer general questions concerning use of various weapons, equipment, etc. Now, whatever you might think, there is not a lot on a 'farty tank landing craft' for members of the public to see and Caen is a large city with lots of inquisitive inhabitants. Once you have climbed aboard, gazed into the empty tank deck, walked aft around the stern by the big kedge anchor, up the other side of the ship, around the fo'c'sle and back, you have just about completed the tour. Living quarters and machinery spaces are, quite naturally, out of bounds to visitors. After all, who would want strangers wandering around their house?

That afternoon, it being 'ship open to visitors', the duty watchmen changed into their 'number three' blue serge suits and manned the various points on deck where they could best keep the traffic moving, ensure that no one came to any harm or strayed out of bounds and answer any questions that they may be asked. In any other circumstances this was a much-sought-after duty that attracted lots of volunteers, as you could get to chat up the girls before anyone else had a chance to. But this being France, there was no queue for the job and so the task fell entirely to the duty watch. Those of us who were not involved stayed in the mess, as few went ashore so early in the day. Billie, Ginger and I were busy preparing our kit ready for a parade we were to participate in at Rouen in a couple of days' time. One or two played 'Chase the Pisser', better known as 'Hearts', while several others were engaged in a particularly noisy game of 'Uckers.' The rest either sat or lay about reading. It was an extremely warm day and so we had the *scuttles* (ports) open. Four of these, two either side of the mess, opened on to the main deck on either side of the ship. Each scuttle was equipped with a side, hinged glass porthole. In addition, each was also equipped with a top-hinged, solid-steel *deadlight*. First the glass porthole was closed and screwed tightly shut, then, if required, the deadlight could be lowered, covering the porthole and screwed tightly shut also. This was done to prevent light either entering or escaping during *action stations* or whenever else the ship's watertight integrity was deemed to be endangered and, in time of war, to prevent shell-splinters penetrating through the glass.

It was therefore quite easy, or dare I say instinctive, for visitors to stop and look through these opened scuttles and into our mess. It was like living in a house with no front garden in a street where passers-by stop to look in at you through your open front window. To begin with, it was not really a problem and pleasantries were exchanged on both sides in 'Froglish' but during the course of the afternoon it became more and more irritating. We tried closing the scuttles but it became far too stuffy for that. Eventually, one particularly obnoxious visitor, displaying a huge Gaullist nose and booze fuelled breath, poked his head in through a scuttle and kept it there for rather longer than we thought appropriate. He was clearly happy to survey the scene and shout unintelligible phrases at us.

"Yeah! Yeah!" we replied.

"Parlez vous to you too, Pierre. Remember Agincourt? Well bugger off and leave us in peace."

Would he take the hint? Not a bit of it. He kept repeating, in very broken English, "You have rum? You and me drink rum together, Oui?"

"Bugger off Pierre!" shouted Yorky, tiring of his persistence and angrily gesticulating to him to leave us in peace. Pierre just scowled back and then spat in Yorky's direction. At that, Mad

Jock raised himself from his game of Uckers and went over to the second of the two scuttles on that side of the mess. It was situated a couple of metres further along the deck and forward of the one that Pierre was peering through. He stood on one of the bench seats, unclipped the heavy steel deadlight hinged above the open scuttle and held it up with one hand, at the same time pressing his body as close up to the bulkhead as possible, so as not to be seen. At the given sign, Yorky indicated that Pierre should go along to the next scuttle and look through, where he would get a good 'gulpers' for his trouble. This Pierre did, exactly as scripted. As his nose, followed by the rest of his head, entered the open scuttle in anticipation, Mad Jock slammed down the deadlight from above. The result was a frightful "Agghhhh!" sound from the throat of Pierre as he reeled off backwards and out of earshot. Mad Jock lifted the deadlight slightly to see a crowd gathering around Pierre, who was now lying flat on his back.

Rushing over to see for myself, I said, "How does he look Jock?" thinking that he may have killed the poor guy.

"He looks like he's just stood a bit too close to a tube of fucking lipstick," grinned Jock.

Amongst much fuss and accusing fingers pointed in the direction of our messdeck, the unfortunate fellow was taken to the Coxswain's office, which, doubled as the sickbay in *Rampart*. There, he was treated to the usual two codeine tablets, gauze, iodine and – would you credit it? – a large tot of rum. About an hour later, a very angry Swain led Pierre into the mess, in the vain hope that he would be able to identify the naval surgeon who had done such a good job in rearranging his nose. He looked pitiful and clearly had problems seeing straight, because he could not identify a soul. Anyway, he had got his tot of rum. Getting no joy whatsoever, the Swain led him out of the mess, to a rousing cheer from us all. He was put in a taxi and accompanied to the local hospital outpatients department by the Swain himself

Upon the Swain's return from the hospital, both Yorky and the Mad Jock were called to his office. The next day at Captain's Defaulters they were jointly charged with behaviour likely to endanger the *Entente Cordiale* and deprived of leave for the rest of our stay in France.

We used to say to them that they must have the best bank account in the world; there were so few opportunities for them to go ashore and spend their money. How the Swain was able to pinpoint the pair of them, we never knew, but then again, it didn't take the Brain of Britain to deduce who was likely behind any plot aboard *Rampart*.

Immediately after defaulters, we sailed from Caen and on to Rouen. It was here that we paraded ashore with other Navy units, Army and Royal Marines, to mark the anniversary of the D-Day landings and to pay our respects to the fallen. The Royal Marines provided the guard. Following a short but poignant service, a minute's silence was observed and wreaths were laid at the memorial in the city centre. That afternoon I and several others travelled to the immense war cemetery outside Rouen. It was a most evocative and moving experience. Although I had heard of the war graves at Ypres, and Mons, I had never been there and so had not been confronted with the human consequences of war on the scale that I viewed before me at that cemetery. Row upon row of white crosses stretched for almost as far as the eye could see in all directions. They stood proudly in the most beautifully maintained gardens imaginable. I walked along the rows for what seemed like hours, stopping to read the names on the crosses and the units to which the fallen had belonged.

At that moment I thought to myself, how could this have ever been permitted to happen? All these young men and women, their lives cut short because people who should have known better were either unable or unwilling to settle their differences in a civilized manner. That afternoon left an impression upon me that remains as vivid today as it was then. I also remember thinking at the time that it should be compulsory for all schoolchildren to visit at least one war cemetery before they leave school, as a reminder of what can happen in a society where people become disenfranchised, acquiescent or just too bone idle to hold their leaders to account. It was also the first time that I consciously mistrusted the word of politicians. I am enraged now when I see turnouts of only 60% or so at election time but, given the record of many of our politicians, I am not really that surprised.

Before leaving Rouen, four of us received permission to visit Bayeux and the world famous tapestry. I was very impressed with it. Imagine how very disappointed I was recently, to find out that the Bayeux Tapestry is not really a tapestry at all, but is embroidered. Ah well, you live and learn.

The day following our tapestry visit, we departed Rouen for Portsmouth to begin our preparations for sailing north. During the journey back across the Channel, Mad Jock McConachy was banned from playing Uckers again in *Rampart*. Uckers, I should add, is a Naval version of Ludo but slightly more complicated and infinitely more heated. It is played with two dice instead of one and, usually, two players sharing red and green counters team up to defeat and humiliate, wherever possible, another two players sharing blue and yellow counters. 'Sixies', 'blobs', 'mixie-blobs', double, triple, four and off! are commonplace terms on a Naval messdeck. That particular night, Mad Jock, together with his young partner, the recently joined stoker who was still learning the game, had managed to get themselves into a brilliant winning position in one of the games in progress at the time.

In what appeared to have been a 'gross failure to pay due attention to detail', the young stoker made an elementary error by creating a mixie-blob out of a clean-blob, thus enabling their opponents to swipe seven of their blue and yellow counters off the board in one sweet move and, in the process, be assured of winning the game.

Mad Jock, enraged by the young stoker's naivety, lifted the long mess table, complete with board and counters, into the air and hurled it across the mess. He then chased the terrified stoker out of the door and onto the upper deck, threatening to serve him the largest 'Rectumectomy' permitted under NATO rules when he caught up with him. Scouse, Pony Moore and half a dozen more of us followed, hoping to prevent a major catastrophe, whilst at the same time inwardly praying that Mad Jock would not, in turn, direct his aggression upon us, as he was quite capable of doing. The stoker, as it happened, was rather more nimble than Mad Jock and shot along the starboard walkway and down into the engineers' store, where he barricaded himself in for the rest of that night. After Jock had calmed down, several of us tried to entice the stoker out but he would not budge. His squeaky voice, penetrating several layers of steel, wood and cartons of cotton waste, told us that he valued his virginity more than he did the words of his new mess-mates. In the morning, the Chief ERA was informed of the stand-off, at which point he went and extricated the poor chap personally from his self-imposed prison. The incident was kept from the eyes and ears of the Swain, on the promise to the Chief ERA by Leading Stoker Pony Moore that he would guard the young lad with his life and that Mad Jock would never be permitted to partner the young lad again at any game. After that incident, we young ones all held our breath come evening time, hoping Jock would not ask any of us to partner him at Uckers. In the event, his ban was withheld without any of us being put on the spot by him. Only Yorky would partner him after that.

A couple of years after this incident, whilst in another ship, I heard via the grapevine that an Able Seaman McConachy had been admitted to the military mental hospital at Netley, near Southampton, apparently on the grounds of 'diminished responsibility'. It was reported that he had walked an imaginary dog around the quarterdeck of HMS *Sheffield*, inviting it to piss up against the Chief Gunnery Instructor's leg each morning during both watches of the hands. It was further reported that a good mate of his, probably Yorky Halliday, had been the first to visit him in Netley Hospital several weeks after his admittance.

Whilst they were in private conversation, Jock is alleged to have said to his mate, "There is sod all wrong with me, shipmate. I was pulling the old dog trick to *earn my ticket* (get early release from the Navy) but I think I went over the top a bit and now they think I really do have a mental problem. You know me better than that, mate, and you must tell them that I am OK really. You are the only hope I have of getting out of here. I rely upon you."

Yorky told him not to worry, he would talk with the doctors at the first opportunity and at the same time spread the word around the messdecks that Jock McConachy was OK really and had only been trying to work his ticket. Upon leaving, Mad Jock walked with Yorky as far as he was permitted, the perimeter of the car park. They bade each other farewell, then Yorky walked alone the forty odd meters to where his old Ford Consul was parked. As he put the key in the door, a house brick came hurtling through the air and smashed into the windscreen. Yorky jumped back and looked up, aghast. There, behind the perimeter fence, was Mad Jock, waving his arms frantically at Yorky and shouting, "Don't forget shipmate, you tell them there is nothing wrong with me, alright?'

6.   There's Moose in My Stew Again

The Pusser's Egg

It stared at me with steady sight,
It's oval body smooth and white,
Movement fluid, deft, with ease,
It's lower body sheathed in grease.
I slashed at it with silvern steel,
A wound appeared then seemed to heal,
It quivered at the blows I ranged,
The structure crumbled, colour drained,
Its eye transfixed me; it seemed to beg,
"Please don't eat this pusser's egg."

   N Art Bruen

Part of our preparations for the Norway visit involved clearing
out and repainting the troop mess deck, the first sign we had
received that we would be embarking troops on this trip. This
mess was down below and just aft of the main engines. It
spanned the width of the ship and was about 35 feet in length. It
was, by a long stretch, the most uncomfortable and noisy
compartment in the ship. Vibration was so bad, when the ship
was underway, that those sleeping on camp beds on the deck
were shuffled like playing cards from one side to the other
during the course of the night. In the morning, its inhabitants
would be in a pig's orphan of a tangle. Besides the camp beds,
there were twenty or so *swinging cots*. These were narrow beds
with side rails and were suspended from the deck *head* [ceiling].
The mess accommodated thirty men maximum. The overflow, if
any, slept within their vehicles on the tank deck.

   The last weekend before sailing northward, I visited home for
one more short weekend – Saturday lunchtime until seven
thirty Monday morning. We were due to sail on the Monday

morning at ten o'clock. I had wanted to go to Birmingham because I loved driving my car and had not really had the opportunity to do so that often. At around five thirty on the Monday morning, during my return journey, the engine of my MG seized up on the A34, just north of Winchester. By disengaging the gears, I managed to push the car along to a darkened lay-by, by which time I was well and truly puffed out. The engine would not turn over, so I lifted the bonnet but I could not see a thing. Furthermore, the road, at that time of the morning, was empty.

"Bugger it!" I said out loud in frustration. "I have to be aboard in two hours' time and I will be away for at least a couple of months. What the hell do I do? If I had gone by coach or rail, or even not at all, I wouldn't be in this God awful mess."

As the car did not lock, I scribbled a note and tucked it behind the wiper blade, then, with my holdall in my hand, I started walking towards Winchester. My note just said 'AB BARR, HMS RAMPART. BROKEN DOWN. WILL COLLECT' The dawn was just breaking when, providentially for me, having walked only half a mile or so, two guys in a Wolseley Twelve came by and picked me up. It transpired that they, like me, were returning from weekend leave and were going to Whale Island. I was so relieved.

As we drove, I told them of my woes and got them to stop briefly in Winchester, where I scribbled another note and popped it through the letterbox of Wadham Stringers, BMC dealers. My note said briefly, 'Car abandoned on A34 three miles north of town, will ring you before nine o'clock.' Before taking leave of my lift, outside Unicorn Gate, I gave the driver the address in Portsea where I was to leave my car whilst away. The address had no telephone, so I could not inform them of my predicament before I left. I then ran through the dockyard and scrambled aboard *Rampart* with just minutes to spare before leave expired.

I waited patiently in the queue to use the only phone in the ship, which was at the gangway. Eventually my turn came but I could get no answer from Wadham Stringers. Answerphones were not then widely in use, so I went to the back of the queue. Before my turn came around again, the phone was disconnected and we began to prepare for sea.

It was midway through June and, having stored ship the previous week, we slipped and sailed out once more into the Solent, heading east towards Dungeness, then northwards up through the North Sea, bound first for Kristiansand and then Narvik. That afternoon I wrote a letter to the friend where I was to have left my car and another to Wadham Stringers, explaining the situation and trusting that they would do everything in their power to recover my car. By then we were well out to sea of course, so I was not able to post them until our arrival in Kristiansand the following week. I heard nothing in return from either of them.

I returned to Wadham Stringers at my first opportunity, two and a half months later, to find no trace of my beloved MG. No one remembered seeing it nor receiving my letter. I could find neither of the two good Samaritans that had given me a lift back to the ship, they having been drafted to other ships during the intervening period. Of the friend who was to look after the car for me, there was no trace. He had also received a draft and had moved his family on as well. That's just how the Navy worked. I never saw the car again, although I kept the logbook for years afterwards. I still retain very fond memories of that little sports car.

Having passed eastwards along the English Channel on one previous occasion only, I was amazed at the amount of traffic that each day passes up and down and across that stretch of water. With the galley door opened onto the port quarter, we could look out at the ever changing scene as we worked. I say 'we' – I could, anyway. From where the Leading Cook was, there was no chance, he being in his usual misery.

The second evening out from Portsmouth, I badly burned the supper. Such was the changing scenery as we rounded the North Foreland that I stood gazing out of the galley door more than I did gazing into the giant cook pot full of mutton stew that was brewing on the galley range. When it came to serving it, I saw how badly I had 'cocked it up'. The top half of the contents of the pot were OK but further down it was ghastly; really and truly horrible. It got progressively thicker and blacker the deeper I went with the ladle. I thought to myself, 'Shit! What do I do now? I can't undo what I've already done.' With seemingly no way out, my belligerence took hold of me once more.

"Oh well, Bollocks!" I shouted loudly out of the galley door at a passing coaster. I set to, skimming off the top two or three inches from the pot for the wardroom mess and arranged it in the smaller serving tray with a forest of mint leaves for decoration. "There, that's nice." I said out loud. I dug a little deeper and filled the next tray for the Senior Ratings Mess. "Stuff them old buggers, they don't matter, add a bit more mint, yeah that's not so bad at all," I said gleefully. Then, looking at what was left for the rest of the ship's company, I said, "Oh my God, look at that! I'll never get out alive if I take that into the mess." I pondered for a moment or two, then I had a brainwave. "I know what I'll do... Cheesy-Hammie-Eggie,' I said to myself, 'That's what I'll do.'

Putting the two trays I had already served up into the warming oven, I worked like a monkey on a banana boat, knocking up the alternative dish for twenty hungry and expectant mouths. The two trays of stew were collected by the respective mess stewards and then Ginger came in for the junior ratings tray.

"There you are Ginger," I said, handing him the tray, "just look at that, fresh from the grill, a meal fit for a king."

First he looked down at the tray's contents, then at me, shook his head slowly from side to side, then turned and left. I was busy scrubbing down when, a few moments later, Scouse, the Leading Hand of the Mess, walked into the galley, demanding an explanation.

"Where the fuck is our mutton stew, young Barr?" He said in an authoritative voice.

I looked everywhere but into his eyes, then, when I could avoid him no longer, I decided to come clean. "Well Scouse, I'm afraid I cannot deny it," I stammered. "I've made a right Cornish cowpat out of supper tonight and no mistake. I have no excuse whatsoever. Look here..." I showed him the pot. "Look how it turned out. There must be a fault on the oil burner."

He took the big pot from the galley range and looked inside, then put his finger deep into the black, sludgy mess, scooped a sample and popped it into his mouth. Looking up at me he said, "Eeerh Whacka, what's wrong with that?" Whereupon he turned and went forward with it to the mess and that was the end of that.

"I have learned a salutary lesson this week," I observed to myself afterwards. Honesty was the best policy. I was about to go into the mess and demand the Cheesie-Hammy-Eggy back, thinking I could reheat them for breakfast, but thought better of it. Later on, when we gathered on the after deck as we often did for a chinwag and our two cans of warm beer each, comments were passed as to how tasty the scran had been that evening. "Some are easily pleased," I breathed easily to myself.

Northwards we crept, at around 12 knots, pretty well the most comfortable speed possible. Anything above this shook the ship and its complement to bits and sleep would be impossible. The early summer weather was fine and visibility hazy as we passed Sheerness and Cromer. Even Dolly responded to the glass-like surface of the sea by resuming command of the galley. I was overjoyed to see him back but in return received a bollocking for ruining his mutton stew.

Ships of all shapes and sizes passed us and, in keeping with maritime etiquette, merchantmen dipped their ensigns to us as they passed. In larger ships, it is the job of the duty signalman to return the salute. In *Rampart* the duty fell to anyone who happened to see the ensign of a passing merchantman lowered. I would often look out of the galley door and see a ship passing by with its ensign at the rail. I would immediately drop whatever I was doing, leap into the bathroom and, if no one else had done so, lower and then raise the white ensign in response. At sea, ships' ensigns remained raised at the staff during the night. In harbour, ensigns were raised in the morning at sunrise and lowered again promptly at sunset.

We had got into trouble with the Officer of the Guard in Portsmouth on many occasions for having our ensign fluttering from the ensign staff long after sunset, everyone having forgotten to lower it. Eventually, we got one of the stokers to drill a hole in the deck head of the junior rates bathroom. The deck above was the one you stood on to raise and lower the ensign. Through the hole, we passed the ensign halyards and secured them to one of the shower taps. Thereafter, anyone using the shower at around sunset lowered the ensign to the deck. In the morning, the exercise was reversed. We never again got into hot water with the Officer of the Guard and at sea, we could use the bathroom to raise or lower the ensign in salute to passing ships.

We passed ships from the Baltic, loaded high with timber; how they could see where they were going was unfathomable. Lovely Dutch coasters throbbed past, their bridge windows a mass of geraniums and lobelia. Whole families lived on these lovely little craft and kept them spotlessly clean. Rusty little colliers, belching black smoke, chugged southwards from North Shields and the Tyne. A few splendid sailing barges and schooners glided silently by, like phantoms shrouded by the sea mist. This scene later inspired me to write the poem 'Coastwise'.

On the fourth or fifth day out, we came to the entrance of the Kattegat and thence the Baltic Sea. I relieved the lookout at four in the morning for the first of my two, one-hour stints. He passed to me the bearings of visual contacts that had already been reported to the Officer of the Watch, after which he left to go below. All but one of these contacts were ships' navigation lights. The one that was not, a flashing white light, was on a bearing of approximately zero seven five degrees, or at about two thirty, if our heading was twelve o'clock. As time passed, the lights of the various ships changed position relative to our course and speed whereas the flashing white light, a marker buoy, maintained its position. When I was relieved, an hour later, I reported all lights to my relief and went down to the galley to make the *Ky* [thick pusser's chocolate] for those on watch and to make preparations for breakfast. At six am, with the dawn breaking, I relieved the lookout again.

The general scene, of course, had changed but to my surprise the flashing white light was where it had been when I had left the bridge an hour before. It was still there when I was relieved again at seven. Indeed, it remained abreast to starboard for most of the morning, only very slowly moving aft, so strong was the tidal flow against us, combined with our flat bottom and puny engines. Eventually, around lunchtime, we left it far astern of us.

About ten that evening, Scouse came into the mess and announced 'Special Sea Dutymen' to the crewmembers who had to man the engine room, bridge, wheel, berthing wires and hawsers when entering or leaving harbour. We were about to enter Kristiansand. Those of us not involved continued to play cards or Ukkers, to read or to turn in and, a couple of hours or so later, the ship secured alongside the small harbour wall. Those involved in the manoeuvre then cleared up and went below, leaving only the duty Quartermaster at our small brow. Before long, we were all in the land of nod.

Bang! Bang! Bang! came the rapping on the door, then, as it opened, on went the lights and Wakey! Wakey! Wakey! you lucky fellows, Special Sea Duty men up quickly NOW!"

Blinking and shielding our eyes from the sudden glare, we peered at each other and at the 'voice at the door.' It was the Quartermaster, hotly pursued by the Coxswain, hastily pulling-on his sea jersey.

"Come on lads, on deck now and make it quick," he added.

Mad Jock was the first to respond. "Jesus Christ Swain! It's only four thirty, what's going on?"

But the Swain had gone up to the wheelhouse.

Those required tumbled out and dressed with haste. This did not involve me or a good many others, so we just lay wondering what the panic was all about or turned over and went back to sleep.

Someone shouted at Mad Jock as he disappeared through the door, "Blow the lights out and tread quietly, you peasant."

"Up yas noses yas wankers!" drifted back to us as the door swung shut.

I fell back to sleep to the far-off sounds of voices, wires dragging along the deck and the throb-throb of the engines. Not for long though, because the returning 'Specials' came stamping in a short while later. It was nearly six am and 'Call the Hands' was at six thirty anyway, so there would be no more sleep for us.

"So what was the bloody panic about?" someone asked.

"Why are we at sea?"

"In the fucking wrong place," announced Ginger, getting undressed for a further half an hour in his pit. "That was *Mandal* not Kristiansand."

We looked at each other quizzically. Mandal? That was fifty miles west of Kristiansand by our reckoning.

We ratings never really discovered the reason behind our brief visit to Mandal. The buzz was that the poor Navigator got it badly wrong. Geordie, the QM on watch at the gangway, said that a fellow had come running along the quay shouting something to him in Norwegian. Geordie had woken the Coxswain, who alerted the Jimmy and, after some discussion, he said the Coxswain had told him to call the hands. Several of those on deck during our departure reported that a largish looking ferry boat had been hovering a hundred metres or so off the quay wall, which, when we left, went alongside the berth we had been on.

"That sounds not unlike *The Navy Lark*, Dolly," I said, as we began to put breakfast together.

"Nothing surprises me any more in this ship," countered Dolly, resignedly.

Later on that morning, we entered Kristiansand proper and berthed port side to, on a public quay. It reminded me very much of Poole Harbour. That evening, leaving only the few watchmen aboard, the remainder of us got changed into our best number one suits and made our way ashore. Kristiansand was a very attractive town with many buildings constructed of wood and painted bright yellow, powder blue or deep copper red. The weather was fine and the people there seemed to be just emerging from the long Scandinavian winter. What struck us most of all was the genuine zest for life exhibited by the local townsfolk. It was the same wherever we went in Norway. I was captivated by it. Neither had I ever seen so many people riding bicycles in my life, real sit up and beg monsters.

There was, however, one major drawback for us sailors, whose first visit this was to the land of the midnight sun. No pubs! Nowhere! Anywhere! It was patiently explained to us by a group of well-meaning natives we encountered, that in Scandinavia the cost of alcohol was very expensive and it was only sold via the state run monopoly, *Systemabolaget* [off licences] or in restaurants and hotels.

"Christ alive!" said Mad Jock, "this looks like it's going to be a run ashore to end all runs ashore and we're up here for over a month! Where is the nearest cheap hotel then?" With directions memorised, we bid them farewell and breezed off to our quarry, a reasonable looking hotel with a small bar.

"OK lads, let's have ten bob each into the kitty. Beers, yes?" called Billie Addison – and beers it was.

While the rest of us waited, we chaffed and talked amongst ourselves about things that generally concern sailors, in this case, blue-eyed, blonde-haired Scandinavian beauties and no pubs to meet them in or to take them to. We had already spotted more of them, blondes that is, in the time it had taken us to get from the ship to the hotel, than we ever thought lived on the planet – and all of them Anita Ekberg lookalikes.

"What! Shave a Snake! We only want to buy beer, not the hotel!" Exclaimed the normally unexcitable Billie Addison from the bar, when told how much the round had cost. It was Friday night and the clock showed eight fifteen. This bar was our first port of call that evening and we were down to a quarter of our spending power after just the first round. To cap it all, they were not even pints! We went into a huddle. Someone suggested asking the barman where we might drink a little more cheaply. This was done by Yorky Halliday and we subsequently discovered, to our dismay, that we were already there. We would find nowhere cheaper in town, so we huddled again.

"Ask him what his cheapest drink is," someone else suggested. Good idea, we agreed. Back came the answer, "Vermouth".

"Ver-bloody-what?" asked Yorky loudly.

We looked askance at each other, none of us having ever heard of the stuff before.

"Never heard of it, but if it's cheaper than this lager piss then we'll have it, was Mad Jock's reply.

When it eventually arrived, it turned out to be most disappointing; small and sweet and not at all sailor-like. Two rounds of Vermouth and the kitty was spent, so we started to split up. Ginger, Yorky, Jock and a couple of others decided to chance their luck elsewhere. The remainder of us strolled around the town for an hour or so and then made our way back to the ship. It was nearly ten o'clock and still light. We changed out of our best uniforms, got out the cards and Ukkers boards and passed away the rest of the evening much the same as if we had been at sea. Most of us were turned in by the time the remainder came off shore at about one in the morning. They were pretty well pissed and woke us sleepers up, clattering about in the dark as they groped around, stowing their gear. It happened that they had been befriended by a group of vodka-drinking alkies at the entrance to a municipal park. Those guys had a stash of Vodka, Polish Spirit and other equally explosive concoctions, which they had been willing to share for a small consideration; that being duty-free cigarettes. So a deal was done and everyone was a winner, as they say.

The next day being Saturday, the Swain, having first conferred with Dolly, set off into town to order some victuals with which to top-up our dry and frozen stores. After dinner, most of the crew, including Dolly Gray himself, went off in search of *rabbits* [gifts, souvenirs]. The remainder of us set to dhobying clothes, ironing or generally relaxing. Most fell asleep.

At about four or so that afternoon, a refrigerated lorry rolled up along the quay and came to a halt abreast the bottom of the gangway. The duty QM poked his head through the port side scuttle and said calmly, "Hey lads, pull your fingers out and get a load of this. There's a meat delivery here, and it needs sorting out."

'That was quick,' we thought, having seen the Swain depart only a few hours earlier. The four of us that were awake in the mess followed the QM out to the short gangway. We stopped dead as our eyes caught sight of two fellows struggling to carry half a carcass of something from the back of the lorry. They huffed and puffed up the gangway, stepped onto the narrow deck and lowered it onto the deck, so that it stood on its truncated legs, propped against the bulkhead. It was half of a complete carcass, cut in half lengthwise top to bottom. It had two legs, a rump, underside and neck, and it stood around five feet high on its stumps.

We stood looking at each other for what seemed ages, no one knowing quite what to say. The QM broke the silence at last, saying simply, "What is it, anyone know?"

"Elk! Please sign here," the driver said in broken English, thrusting a docket in front of the QM.

"Not me, him," said the QM, pointing at me. I shuffled backwards, wanting no part in signing for anything. I had signed for a bike in Barracks once and ended up painting white spots on the parade ground for the rest of the week. Why? Because I was foolish enough to have signed a chit without looking at what I was signing for. Eventually, the QM put his signature where shown, after which the delivery men bade farewell and departed.

"Well, what are you going to do with that, Cookie mate?" asked the QM sarcastically. "You can't leave it there. For one thing it's blocking the way, secondly, it looks untidy and thirdly, it'll melt."

The ship had a freezer, measuring about six feet in height by four feet by four feet. Access to it was down through one of the small hatches in the port walkway leading forward. After a few minutes consideration, we decided to break out the tools from the damage control locker housed in the Engineer's Store.

"Where is the bloody Swain?" I asked the QM.

"Knowing our Swain, he's probably in some den of iniquity drinking the health of the Viking Lords of Norway with the butcher that sold him this... this *moose*. He'll not be back aboard this side of midnight, you can bet your life on that."

When the leading cook might return, I had no idea. The Navigator was Officer of the Day but he would be about as much help as a tube of cornflakes in a situation like this. Frozen Moose was not going to be up his street on a Saturday afternoon. No, we were going to have to sort it ourselves.

"I know what we must do, break it into manageable pieces somehow, so that we can stow it away into the deep freeze," I said. Just then, the Duty Stoker turned up with two axes and a large saw and I went off with Geordie to fetch up the shot mat from the Bosun's Store. Upon our return, we laid the thick coir matting on the deck and then the carcase on top of it.

The visit of our ship to Kristiansand had caused some interest amongst the local townspeople. Berthed as we were on a public quay, many of them had taken to walking along the quay to look down at us. Sometimes up, but mainly down as we were not so big a craft. Whilst working we had engaged them in conversation, particularly if they asked us questions about our ship. This being a fine Saturday afternoon, there were more promenaders than usual walking on the quay. When we had assembled the gear we needed, the four of us looked at each other as would a group of first year student surgeons, not knowing quite where to make the first incision. Geordie broke the silence by suggesting we start from the top.

"Good idea, Geordie," I said, and with that, the Duty Stoker took hold of the saw and tried to separate the head from the body.

Well, he would have had more success trying to sink the *Bismarck* with a clockwork dildo. The moose carcase was frozen solid and the teeth of the saw made no impression on it whatsoever. There was a spontaneous outbreak of ideas from those on the quay, whose numbers had gradually swollen to twenty or so.

"I could go and get a blow torch and soften it up a bit," the duty Stoker said, throwing the saw to one side.

"No, you'd melt the bloody thing," said the QM.

"Look you two, hold it tight, I'll see if the axe works better," I said, impatiently. I picked the implement up, raised it over my head, shut my eyes and brought it crashing down somewhere around the neck area. No one was quite sure exactly where because, as it connected with the frozen carcase, bone splinters, gristle and bits of frozen meat flew in all directions. Those that had not already done so before, had instinctively closed their eyes as the axe head met the moose. The result, however, was that we had at least succeeded in separating the head from the body... well almost.

"A good start that was, judging by the applause from the quay," said the QM loftily.

With more turning up each minute to watch the spectacle, we whacked and smashed and broke the thing up into pieces. An hour or so later, the job done, we stood back, wiping our brows and viewed our handiwork. It wasn't exactly pretty – more like an entry for the Turner Prize – but it was effective. The applause from the quay was generous. All in all, we took down and packed into the freezer, a dozen or more chunks of frozen moose carcase and two buckets of splintered bits besides, although there was not one piece among them that looked like anything you would see in a butcher's window. By the time we had finished, the freezer was crammed to capacity. With the show over, the crowd on shore slowly dissolved, moving off in the direction of the town. We, meanwhile, set to work on the iron deck and bulwarks with buckets and scrubbers, restoring them to their normal spotless condition.

When the Swain came off shore that night he admitted to having had a few drinks but could not recall buying the moose. This worried the hell out of the QM, who had signed for it. The Swain had though, he said, arranged a football match the following day between the ship's company and a local youth club. The butcher, it turned out, was the youth club leader and the Swain, clearly under the influence, had thought it a good idea to pit the might of the Royal Navy against the youth of the town. He told Scouse to organise a team for the next day. When it was pointed out to him that we had no equipment in the ship, he simply responded by suggesting that *Rampart* play in blue overalls. What a prat! Only three of us had football boots, so the remainder had to play in either seaboots or engine room steaming boots.

We arrived at the venue next morning at eleven, to find a couple of hundred of the local townsfolk lining the touchlines. "Bloody Coxswain," said Billie to me, "He's nowhere to be seen as usual. He needs a right kick up the arse."

The surface of the pitch was quite damp and for 45 minutes or so, those in overalls and balaclavas, skidded around the pitch on their arses, trying to wrest the ball from eleven very talented youngsters, clad in the very latest football strip. With the score hovering around twelve nil against and four of the bystanders coming on to help us out, the referee asked our captain, Ginger, what he wanted to do to even the game up a little more.

"Get fucking pissed mate," he replied forcefully.

With that not an option here, we mutually agreed to end the farce and return aboard ship. We took the opposition and our four extras with us, showed them around the ship and then treated them all to sippers at tot time. They were delighted. We told the Swain, quite forcefully, to organise darts in future not football.

On Monday morning we departed Kristiansand for Narvik although at that precise moment, none of us were aware that we were about to undertake the trip of a lifetime, a trip that people today pay thousands of pounds for, a journey up the Norwegian fjords.

Once out of the harbour we encountered a good blow from the west, which later that day sent Dolly to his bed again. But not before he had created a superb moose stew for supper that evening. It had to be moose stew, because the moment we opened the freezer door the night before, it all fell out on top of us.

"We need to deplete this a little," he said, pulling out a particularly ghastly sculptured chunk, which he immediately recognised to be a foreleg.

My regard for him grew even stronger, he being able to determine that from the shattered wodge he held up in his hand. He had already learned what had occurred the Saturday before and had had a good old go at the Swain over it. Before they had proceeded ashore that day, they apparently had agreed on cut joints. The buzz went around that the Swain was offered a better deal, including drinkies, if he bought the whole carcass frozen. The amount of stew made from the joint that afternoon was far in excess of what could be eaten for supper that day, so, there being no sign of Dolly the following morning, I decided to boil a little more moose meat up and to add that, with some carrots and turnips, to the remainder of the previous day's supper.

Bingo! Dinner sorted out for Tuesday without breaking into a sweat. There were one or two caustic remarks made over dinner about the similarity between Monday's supper and Tuesday's dinner, but nothing for me to get upset about. The problem was that I had made too much again by far. Either that or they were eating less; it was, admittedly, very rich food. I went down to see Dolly that afternoon to ask for his advice but he was out for the count. I thought to myself, *if only I can clear this we can start afresh tomorrow with the chicken fricassee, that was meant to be on tonight's menu.* I had noted that the Swain had also brought off shore with him a huge tin of Knorr Beef Gravy or stock powder. We had never seen such a thing before. *Maybe I can disguise tonight's supper a little...* I remember thinking. *I will also do roast potatoes instead of mash – that should help head off a potential mutiny...*

So for supper and the third meal in a row, we had moose stew number three, heavily disguised as beef stew and roast potatoes. I had opened, in readiness, two five-pound tins of Bartlett's pears in syrup for afters. The stew was taken away by the various mess men without too much fuss.

I went forward to the Junior Ratings Mess and joined my shipmates for supper. I had been seated only minutes when the Wardroom Steward put his head around the door and beckoned me outside. When we got into the passageway he said to me, "Message from the Wardroom Mess. The Captain sends his compliments to the cook but there is a Moose in his stew again. If there is nothing else to eat on this ship, can you find some way of jazzing it up without trying to make it look like beef?" He handed back to me, the tray of stew, exactly as I had given it him. There were also loud murmurs coming from behind the Senior Rates Mess door.

Bollocks! I thought. *That wasn't exactly the best idea I ever had.* And with that, I went back into the galley to take stock of matters.

The captain and officers had openly rebelled and were still awaiting their supper. There were rumblings from the three Senior Rates but as yet there was no confrontation. I couldn't tell what was going on in my own mess. I had doused the oil-fired range for the evening, so anything hot was out of the question in the time I had available. Hmmm! Then I did something totally irrational. If my decision to put on stew for the third meal in a row was not the wisest one, my next decision bordered on the reckless. I ladled six pear halves out of the desert tray into the wardroom stew.

Then I called up for the steward. He came in, picked up the tray and looked at it as though it had rabies.

"What's' this?" he asked.

"Venison a la Barr...tlett," I replied, proudly.

"I can't take it up like that! You just can't do this sort of thing for officers."

"Well," I said. "There is nothing else I can do now, apart from scrambled eggs. Perhaps you would like to give the Wardroom the choice?"

Then I relit the galley range, just in case. Off he went, still grumbling, and I returned to my mess. I received some pretty mild abuse from them but rather less than I had expected. I finished my cold meal in silence and, turning to Billie Addison, I remarked, "Mate, I think I am going to be in the shit for this."

Billie just nodded and replied, "Yeah, that's the way I see it too. It's just the way the mop flops, Cookie."

Everyone else in the mess was well into tombola by the time I returned to the galley to scrub out and close it down for the night. On my arrival there I found the Wardroom Steward beating eggs and frying tomatoes. He would not speak to me but I could see that my *Stew a la Bartlett* had not been well received.

"Just make sure you leave everything clean and tidy," I told him before going back to the mess.

Later that evening we entered the calmer waters of Boknafjorden and the Karmsurdet and next morning we awoke to the most amazing scenery any of us had ever seen. We were gliding gently between huge black and grey mountains which tumbled steeply down, either to a narrow green plateau close by the water's edge or into the water itself. Dotted irregularly along the green strips of land were wooden houses of every shape, colour and size – blue, white, yellow, red and grey. It was the most stunning scene I had ever seen in my life. In places, the fjord narrowed to less than two hundred meters. People on shore could be seen going about their business and, here and there, a ferry, linking the islands, crossed in front or behind us. In places, the cliffs were perpendicular and water cascaded from the very top of some of them, casting small rainbows across the fjord in the sunlight. The sky teemed with seabirds of many different kinds, some diving from great heights straight into the water for fish. It was truly magnificent. No one wanted to miss a minute of it. Even Yorky and Mad Jock, neither of whom were easily moved by things of beauty other than the sort of females who frequented the Albany and Lennox, were awestruck by it.

The whole experience was somewhat soured a few hours later when I was reprimanded for my performance at suppertime the previous day. I was formally stood down from Cook's Mate and replaced by Geordie. He was not too pleased at the change but, like me, he was given no choice. The whole mess was unimpressed as well, for Geordie showed little zest for the job of cooking. I took over his duties on deck. Dolly was called up to see the Swain and told to take charge of his galley or face the consequences. Seasickness would not be tolerated in future. Surprisingly, Dolly never held it against me. The Captain, who spoke to me on the bridge whilst navigating a particularly crowded stretch of waterway, told me that my behaviour the night before had bordered on outright insolence. He then dismissed me with a silent wave of his hand. In hindsight, he was absolutely spot-on and it was about the right time for a job change anyway, given that I had never received any formal training as a cook. Had I asked for a change, it would not have been granted, so the end justified the means as I saw it. And I really didn't give a slapper's gusset at the time anyway. I was glad to be out in the open again, doing what I had joined up to do.

So with Geordie in the galley and me on the afterdeck, northwards we journeyed at twelve knots. Sometimes we had land on both sides or, if just off the coast, we had open sea to port. At other times it looked as though we were landlocked, having tall and majestic mountains on either beam and ahead of us. But always the enclosing land opened up to reveal another stretch of open water ahead. The further north we travelled, the more often we transited the longer fjords, which lay northeast/southwest along the coast of Norway. The mountains here were not as high as they had been further south and there were many more skerries and low lying rock formations about but the scenery was still spectacular. It was now light until nearly eleven but by midnight or so, most of us were turned in.

One night we were in the Edoyfjorden, just to the south of Trondheim, passing between the mainland and the large offshore islands of Smola and Hitra. About two in the morning the engines were put suddenly astern and the whole ship vibrated as the screws bit into the water to slow the ship down. After a few minutes of this there was silence, and in the darkness of the mess someone mumbled, "You wait and see... Special Sea Dutymen in five minutes from now."

But no, the throb-throb-throb of the diesels recommenced and we were on our way again but we were turning sharply. That was no longer unusual, we had been twisting and turning through the fjords for three days now. At breakfast in the morning, the Quartermaster of the *middle watch* [midnight to four am] explained what had happened.

"I was on the wheel and the Jimmy was Officer of the Watch. The Jimmy called the Captain, who joined him a few moments later on the bridge. Apparently, there were a number of confusing lights marking the passage ahead. To starboard and up the Tronheimsfjorden, was the port and city of Trondheim. That was not our destination. However, there were several smaller fjords branching ahead and to port of us. It was here that the confusion lay. It being dark, only the flashing lights of marker buoys and the vague outlines of the fjord sides could be seen. After some discussion and consulting the charts, they each had differing opinions, so the Captain then said to the Jimmy, "So be it, Number One, we'll toss up for it. Heads we take your channel and tails mine." The Captain won the toss and so on we went without stopping. Forty five minutes later I got the order 'Stop Both Engines' followed rapidly by 'Half Astern Both Engines'. We had come to the end of Stjorfjorden. That's where we turned around and went back again."

"Glad someone knows where we're bleeding going," said Yorky.

As we drew still further north, so the daylight hours increased. It was now eleven thirty before the sun dropped below the horizon, only to pop up again at one thirty in the morning. The sun shone pretty well every day, radiating a warmth that none of us could comprehend, being as close as we were to the Arctic Circle. Routine went haywire for a while, not the ship's routine, which continued as normal, but personal routines changed enormously. In the evenings, the mess, normally a hive of activity with card schools, Ukkers, Tombola and even the odd film show from time to time, was to be found deserted. The whole crew sat around on the afterdeck and talked, played cards or just took in the ever changing scenery instead. Time passed without people noticing. One such evening Ginger, glancing at his watch, shouted, "Christ Alive! It's nearly two o'clock and I've got to be up at four for the morning watch!"

It seemed that no-one wanted to go below. It was not even getting dark now, just twilight. Four days after leaving Kristiansand we entered the Vestfjorden and the approaches to Narvik, fifty or so miles inside the Arctic Circle. This was sacred ground for sailors of the Royal Navy. We were all aware of the famous battles fought hereabouts during the Second World War, of Captain Warburton-Lee, the Navy's first World War II Victoria Cross recipient and his signal "Keep on engaging the enemy!" as his ship was shot out from under him. Also, of Captain Phillip Vian and his rescuing of the prisoners aboard the German prison ship *Altmark*. The cry from the prisoners of "The Navy's here!" has since become part of British folklore.

It was in the Ofotfjorden that we embarked our DUKW cargo, their crews and Marines. DUKWs' were mobile troop carriers, capable of travelling on land and water.

We were given to understand that a huge exercise was taking place to test NATO's readiness to defend the Northern Flank of Europe against a Soviet incursion. We were to embark and at some point land our DUKWs with the Marines, on the mainland somewhere northeast of the Lofoten Islands. We embarked eight of these floating assault craft and around 120 Royal

Marines. They were with us for three days. The ship suddenly felt extremely cramped. The troop deck was heaving with Marines and the more intelligent of them evacuated it and slept on camp beds amongst, on top of or in their DUKWs. Dolly was handed half a dozen helpers from the embarked personnel and I was drafted back to the galley, temporarily, to assist. There were now so many to cater for and so little space and equipment to work with, that breakfast, dinner and supper were served in three waves. The first breakfast serving was at 5:45, the second at 6:30 and the third at 7:15am. The dinner servings were 11:30, 12:15 and 1pm. Supper was at 6:15, 7:00 and 7:45pm. It was hard work but everyone was fed on time and the quality of the food was unimpaired.

Three days after embarking, our friends – yes, we became very good friends in that short time together – we entered a sheltered inlet with a shingle beach in the distance, somewhere in the vicinity of Bodo, where we waved goodbye to the Marines and their DUKWs. Just prior to these landings, we had encountered some of the other participants in the exercise, in the shape of the depot ship HMS *Adamant*, several destroyers and frigates and two American landing craft. These, I think, were now in the same vicinity as us but were not within sight.

Having completed the first phase of the exercise, we were told that we were to retire to the town of Harstad in the Lofoten Islands, 150 miles inside the Arctic Circle. The following morning we tied up at our berth in the small town. Harstad was a pretty little town full of timber-built houses painted much the same as others we had seen in Norway. There was a predominance of deep red colour here though, probably reflecting the harshness of the arctic winters. Unsurprisingly, there was not a single bar in the town and only two small hotels. Most of the crew decided to stay aboard or just to walk around the few shops that were to be seen. That first evening, a portly gentleman presented himself at the foot of the gangway and told the QM that anyone who wished would be welcome to attend a dance the following evening at the town's social club, the *Folketshus*.

There being no chance of alcohol served, only six or seven of us took up his offer. Fortunately for our Norwegian host, who had been kind enough to extend this invitation, Yorky, Ginger and Mad Jock declined to attend. Those of us who accepted that evening, changed into our number one uniforms and strolled for about a mile up the gravel track, out of the town and into the forest above it. Eventually, we came upon a single-storey wooden building and, sure enough, we heard music emitting from within. On stepping through the door, we doffed our caps and were met by the fellow who had extended the invitation. The room was brightly lit, not artificially, but by the sunlight streaming through the windows. It was surreal. In one corner were a half dozen or so teenagers, crouched over what appeared to be a Dansette record player. In another corner was a long trestle table full of cinnamon buns, doughnuts, biscuits, sandwiches and coffee mugs. The remainder of the hall was taken up by people between the ages of eight and eighty, either sitting or standing in groups, chatting. Upon our entry, everything seemed to stop. People turned and looked at us quizzically. Never before had I felt so self-conscious. This state of mortification lasted but a few moments only.

"Come on in, welcome to our folkets evening. Where are you all from?"

We were assailed from all sides. Never was I made more welcome in a strange place as I was that evening. We were bombarded with questions.

"Where do you come from? Have you ever seen the Queen? Are any of you from Liverpool? Have you seen any of the Beatles? Have any of you seen Tommy Steele? Would you like some coffee? Come and sit over here with and talk English with us."

My recollections of that evening have not been dimmed by the years. I remember it as though it was yesterday. If I had not already done so on the journey, I fell in love with Norway that night, with Scandinavia in general and with Ingaard in particular. Ingaard was a very beautiful blonde girl of around seventeen. It was love at first sight. I saw her over the top of a cup of wishy-washy coffee, standing by the Dansette with several other local lads and lasses. Everything about her was perfect. She was sylphlike, composed and, as I noticed later, danced like a fairy. There was just one fly in the ointment, however, which I very soon perceived, for although I loved her oh-so-much, I was not the only one to spot her. At least three of my shipmates did also. The rest of the evening was like a chess game, with one or the other of us trying to checkmate the others.

I had several dances with Ingaard. Jiving was in vogue at the time but with such a queue awaiting her favours it was impossible to take more than my allotted share of her time and she was scrupulously fair-minded. All too soon, with the sunlight still streaming through the windows, the evening came to a close and, to our chagrin, Ingaard said goodbye to us all individually, then departed for home with her parents and brothers. Thanking profusely all those with whom we had shared the course of the evening, we strolled in silence back to the ship, each of us deep in our own thoughts.

We were all smitten by the unremitting friendliness and hospitality shown to us by those Lofoten Islanders and Ingaard in particular. Also, we had had a fine time but had not imbibed a drop of alcohol.

Two days later, we singled up and slipped our berth to begin our journey back to the landing beach and our Royal Marine friends. On the quayside to wave us off was Ingaard. She stood there in a cherry red coat, waving until she was lost from sight. We collected the cargo that we had landed four days earlier and turned southwards to commence the long journey home, disembarking the Marines and their DUKWs at Narvik en route. Once this had been accomplished safely, we headed for the open sea and Garelochead on the west coast of Scotland.

The journey back was uneventful, retracing our route as far as Bergen before turning to the south west for a landfall on the northwest coast of Scotland. The weather held fine and once more we all promenaded as we swept down the fjords, gasping at the scenery as we did so. One moment it seemed that there was no way through the land mass all around us, then a gap would appear and beyond it open sea again. It was truly remarkable. I told my mother and father all about it several months later and when father eventually retired, he took my mother and my old BSA 350 and toured the whole of Norway up as far as Bodo. They too fell in love with the country. I thought my father pretty brave at the time, undertaking that journey on an old 1952 motorcycle when he was nearly seventy years of age. It is small wonder, therefore, that today my wife Stephanie and I own a small wooden house just over the border in Sweden, two of our daughters have homes there and one of our sons has lived for nearly twenty years in Finland.

A week after leaving Narvik, we tied up alongside a boom defence vessel in the Gareloch on the west coast of Scotland. We stayed there for only three or four days, which for most of us was quite long enough, as it poured with rain the whole time. The only exceptions were Mad Jock McConachy and Yorky, who went on weekend leave to visit Jock's family in Glasgow. It being by far too great a distance for any of the remainder of us to travel, we turned our attention to the small matter of how we could brighten up inside of our ship.

7.   The Admiral Was Not Amused

From 'Ratlin' Down'

Climb the rigging, spread the canvas,
Now we've left the Horn behind us
And we've left the snow and sleet
Many leagues away.
Now we're in the South Atlantic
And the life is not so frantic,
We'll be redding up tomorrow but
We're ratlin' down today.

> **N Art Bruen/R Barr**

We left the Gareloch for Inverary to partake in another exercise
landing Royal Marines – a brief and fairly unremarkable affair,
apart from the millions of midges that invaded us. We were
plagued by them from the time we beached until we left. It was
amusing to look for'ard at those working the bow doors, the
ramp and in the tank deck. In between turning handles, bot-
tlescrew slips and unclipping vehicles, they danced around,
flailing the air in their demented attempts to rid themselves of
the annoying pests. *What a shame that such a beautiful and
tranquil setting as this could be ruined by such predatory
insects,* I mused to myself. When they bit you, you knew you
had been bitten, small as they were.

On completion, we returned briefly to the Gareloch to refuel.
We were not sorry to leave there the following day. It was a
dismal and forlorn looking place, made all the worse by the rain
and the rows of dead ships moored alongside each other,
awaiting disposal. During evening rounds on one of the days
whilst alongside, the Jimmy had commented upon the state of
the paintwork in messes, *flats* [passageways], bathrooms and
heads. What had once upon a time been gleaming white, was

now a sludgy creamy-brown or dull ochre. The inside of the ship had not been painted during any of the existing crew's time in her.

Jock opened the conversation. "Sir, are we permitted a say in the colour?"

The Jimmy looked thoughtful for a moment or two and then replied, "I should think so, Able Seaman MaConachy, within reason. Perhaps you could talk to the Coxswain about it. But whatever you decide upon, have it completed before we reach Portsmouth next week."

After he had gone, we pretty much forgot about it until the following day. The matter was raised again over breakfast and it was agreed by all present that someone other than Yorky or Jock should go and talk it over with the Swain. Had either of them gone, the answer to whatever they might request would have been an emphatic "No!" There was never any love lost between him and the pair of them. That afternoon Yorky, Billie Addison and I went forward to the Bosun's Store, which doubled as a paint locker. Once inside, we found the usual drums of shipside grey, one of red-lead, a drum of white, some Brunswick Green non-slip deck-paint, several quart tins of various colours for damage control markings and a scruffy old leather football; a paltry choice, to say the least. But we were not going to be deterred by this small setback.

"We can mix some of the damage control paint with the white," Yorky suggested. "Look, there is green, blue or red, we don't want yellow because that will give us what we already have."

"Green'll make you throw up and blue is, well, it's just blue isn't it?" Billie added.

"That's it then," stated Yorky, "it's the red. Billie, you're the best one to go and see the Swain. Tell him that we want 'the very palest of off-white, with a hint of springtime and a blush of summer."

There was stunned silence for a moment as Billie and I looked across at him, unable to believe our ears.

"That's about the most cultured thing you have ever said, Yorky." I said to him. In fact, it was the highest number of words any of us had ever heard him string together in one sentence. Billie, enquired if he had swallowed the mess Scrabble set, to which Yorky, returning to his more familiar character, looked around him, picked up an old six-inch paintbrush and slung it at Billie, who was making a rather rapid exit up the ladder. Fortunately for Billie, the brush missed his head by inches. Yorky then turned to me, saying, "You got anything more to say for yourself?"

I shook my head and kept my silence. I knew better than to antagonise Yorky Halliday in a compartment eight feet square and with just one exit, situated the other side of him.

We had also decided, between us, that the most advantageous time for Billie to tackle the Swain on the small but important matter of colour, would be just after tot time. We knew from experience that the old bugger was most affable for an hour or so after his daily rum intake. So, after lunch, Billie went off to the Swain's cabin with instructions from us not to take no for an answer. He emerged a few minutes later with a broad grin on his face and a thumbs-up. We could paint the living spaces inside the ship the colour we had chosen, commencing Friday, the Swain had said.

Having steamed out of the Firth of Clyde in a rain squall, we encountered better weather when we turned south into the Irish Sea and called briefly at Douglas in the Isle of Man. It was a difficult place to berth, owing to the five-metre tidal difference between high and low water. I was duty QM for the first watch during the first evening in harbour and I spent the whole of my watch either paying out or hauling in the berthing wires. One moment the gangway was almost vertical from the ship's deck up to the quayside. Six hours later, it was the opposite way around. With a rising tide and too much slack left in the berthing wires, the ship would begin to drift away from the quayside, with the prospect of the gangway falling into the harbour. With just one body on the end of a berthing wire, it took ages to get the slack back in. At about eleven that evening, I had to call out the duty watch to lend a hand to get the ship back snugly alongside. My call for help was greeted with, "Bloody baby sailors, can't be left alone for five minutes!"

The same thing happened again during the morning watch, except that this time the ship was almost hanging by its wires. They were as taut as a fiddlers G-string and we had to be extremely careful in paying out some slack or the hawser would have taken charge and payed out with a rush and most likely injured someone. Two nights alongside in Douglas was enough for most of us. As we were forsaking our next Saturday and Sunday to paint ship, the Jimmy gave us a *make-and-mend* [half day off, given originally to make and mend clothes] on the Thursday afternoon.

The weather improved further as we headed southward and soon it was baking hot, with the surface of the sea like a looking glass. We considered it far too nice to loaf about in the mess on our half day off, so, remembering the old football we had seen in the Bosun's store, we seamen decided to challenge the odds-and-sods to a game of football down in the open tank deck. To start with there were some misgivings amongst those able to participate. The surface of the deck was not conducive either to good football or to the physical security of the combatants. But this was long before the namby-pamby days of 'Health and Safety' when we were more carefree, if not more injury free, and having fun was far more important than sustaining a few cuts and bruises. For one thing, there were large eyebolts dotted around the tank deck, for securing whatever vehicles were being transported and preventing them from moving about. In addition, there were circles of steel bolts, an inch and a half high, in a dozen or more places, securing access plates to the bilges. But it was the only space available and if it was good enough for divisions, it was good enough for tank deck football. More to the point, the odds-and-sods could not pass up such an opportunity to get one over on the seamen. We managed, therefore, to rummage up two teams of seven, which, given the dimensions of the tank deck and the watch-keeping requirements, was as many as we could muster.

We seamen volunteered to play in skins, so that we could get a bit of a tan before returning to Portsmouth; the odds-and-sods wore shirts. There being no one else available, the Navigator, who had the afternoon watch on the open bridge above, agreed to referee the game from there. We drew two goalposts with chalk at each end of the tank deck and let play commence with the dropping of the ball into our midst from the bridge above.

The game was rough enough to raise hackles on both sides, was noisy enough to blot out the sound of the referee's whistle and, very soon, it became injurious enough for both sides to pause for breath. By then, we were down to five-a-side. One of our young seamen sprained his ankle and the wardroom steward stubbed his toe against a protruding ringbolt, leaving a trail of blood wherever he went. Ginger got a bad case of deck rash, bruised ribs and a gashed forearm, having been barged into one of the vertical access ladders and poor old Dolly, who had never before been down into the tank deck, was violently seasick, pebble-dashing anyone who passed within range of him. Friend and foe alike, tried to give him a wide berth.

Play was then held up for over half an hour when the ball cannoned off someone and disappeared out of the tank deck, over the ship's side and into the sea.

"Lost ball, suspend play until a replacement is found!" shouted the Navigator through his megaphone, from the bridge above.

"Sir, it's the only one we've got, can't we go and get it?" shouted someone from the tank deck.

The Navigator must have conferred with the Captain, because, a few minutes later, the ship slowed and turned around, heading back for 'Exercise Football Overboard'. It was hoisted back aboard, using a boathook with a fishing net attached to the end.

After resuming our course and speed, the game recommenced with a word of warning from the Captain. "Don't let it happen again. There won't be a second time."

A few minutes later, Yorky barged the odds-and-sods goalie over the line for what was to be the final goal of the day, except that 'the line' was the tank deck ramp, made of solid steel. The goalie, one of the younger stokers, was carried 'lifeless' from the tank deck. The game was conclusively over just minutes later when Mad Jock, having become bored with the proceedings, picked up the ball rugby-style and drop- kicked it far out into the Irish Sea for the second and final time that day.

"You fucking mad bastard Jock!" we all chorused, before climbing disconsolately up onto the sidewalk to watch silently as the ball drifted away astern of us.

The Swain's office looked like a field hospital when, eventually, we lost sight of the ball and trooped by there on the way to our mess for tea. Of all the injuries, the Wardroom Steward's split toe was the worst. It looked like a soggy jam roly-poly as he sat with his leg up on the mess stool that evening. The Senior Rates Messman had to stand in for him in the wardroom for two days, with Geordie looking after the Senior Rates Mess as well as the galley during that time. The young stoker was not that badly damaged and was able to return to his duties the next day, albeit with a bandaged head.

On Friday afternoon we mixed the paint. At least, those of us who were prepared to take the flak afterwards, did. It's amazing where all those with good intentions disappear to when there are hard choices to be made.

"Put the whole fucking tin in or it won't even touch it," I said, as Billie held the tin for all to see. "Look, it's only a quart tin of red, going into a twenty gallon drum of white; we'll be lucky to spot the difference," I concluded.

There being no immediate objections from the four or five faces peering into the drum of white, in it went. The stirring started, just like mixing a cake and, for a short while, things looked really good.

"If it stays like that, it'll be terrific," said a voice from the back. The rest of us muttered our agreement. By and by, a streaky red colour started to come up to the surface.

"Stir faster," I suggested, thinking that the speed of the stir would alter things for the better.

It didn't. It became quite obvious that the finished article was going to be neither lighter nor darker than what we could see before us. Salmon Pink! Not for the first time in my naval career, I heard someone murmur, "You bloody wanker Barr. Explain that one away if you can."

"Oh no, not *Me ... Us!*" I replied vehemently, looking around me at the rest of them. "I didn't touch either of those tins. I only put forward the suggestion."

"We could mix a bit of grey with it," Billie suggested. "It might tone it down a bit. What do you think?"

Failing to agree, we put the top back on the big drum, looked pensively at each other, then scuttled off to our respective areas to prepare the surfaces for painting, which comprised washing down the old paintwork with hot water and soft soap. That evening in the mess, I came in for some stick from the others.

"Wait until the Swain claps his eyes on that tomorrow," warned Ginger.

"You'd better have enough money to buy yourself out after the Jimmy sees it," chipped in Pony Moore.

Saturday morning came and with Captain's Rounds cancelled on account of the 'Big Paint' we broke out the small pots and brushes. The Senior Rates Messman, plus two, were detailed to paint the Senior Rates mess, their heads and bathroom; not a large area, in comparison to the rest. Two of us were detailed to take care of our own bathroom and heads. Two others had the cross passageways and three or four were to attack the Junior Ratings' mess. The Navvi, when asked, declined the offer of having the wardroom painted. The remainder of the crew were watch-keeping in the ship. We brought up the paint drum to the afterdeck and opened it. There were exclamations of disbelief all round.

"What the fuck have you done there? It's Pink!" said someone who had not been at the mixing ceremony.

"It looks like the two cheeks of a baboon's bum today," I muttered, looking at Yorky.

"Looks to me more like a tart's window box," Yorky replied, hotly.

Mad Jock, who by this time was bent over the drum filling the individual pots, looked over his shoulder and grunted between his teeth. "Stop manking you bunch of fishwives and get bloody painting."

This we did, as though our very lives depended upon it. Nobody wanted to be 'caught in the act' so-to-speak. By the time either the Swain or the Jimmy saw the results, it would be too late. We had completed well over half the job before the Swain became the first to witness our handiwork, when he descended from the ship's office on the deck above to his mess at tot time. The Messman said afterwards that when the Swain saw the colour of his mess, he nearly squit a Dreadnought into his pants. One of the stokers said he had heard his roar from the engine room. Minutes later, the Jimmy was at his side, surveying what was left of the old, dirty, creamy-brown and our efforts to improve it. The contrast between the old colour and the sparkly new Salmon Pink was either gorgeous or disgusting, depending upon which side of the divide you stood. We did not need telling that the pair of them were 'unpleasantly surprised' with the colour scheme. We just kept our heads down and got on with the job, avoiding eye contact where possible, so as not to be in any way incriminated. They stood out of hearing distance, with the Jimmy, talking in very animated tones to the Swain. It was clear for all to see that he was quite underwhelmed with the colour scheme and was letting the Swain know that for sure.

During that afternoon and the following day, the Swain, in turn, made it known to us that we had better watch our backs from now on, because he would be looking for every opportunity to save Her Majesty's Government money by curbing our future liberty and travel. Frankly, no-one gave a bishop's bum-tag what he thought but we couldn't tell him that. Apart from that, surprisingly little more was said about it just then. However, on the Monday morning we were told that the ship would be undertaking planned maintenance, in dockyard hands, towards the end of the year and that one of the priorities, now, would be to restore dignity to the inside of HMS *Rampart*. We were not at all impressed by that news, but there it was. At least we would have nearly three months to enjoy our 'tart's window box', as Yorky had so crudely put it.

As we approached the Scilly Isles, before turning to make our way 'Up Channel', we received a boost to our flagging morale. Jock had brought back off shore in Gareloch, a twelve inch black and white television set, which the Leading Electrical Mechanic said he might be able to convert to run on the ship's AC power supply of 110 volts. Unbeknown to the rest of us, he had been working on it for several days and had converted it successfully, so, for the first time ever, we were able to watch BBC and ITV in the Junior Ratings mess. Or rather, I should say, a snowstorm, with lighter and darker shadows racing across the screen. The aerial cable, attached to a metal coat hanger, was dangled out of a scuttle. Every time the ship changed course by a few degrees or so, we lost the shadows and watched just the snowstorm. We were captivated by it and argued for hours about what might actually be happening on the screen. It provided a change from the only other form of broadcast we received, that of the overseas service of the BBC on the radio.

Once again we put into Poole Harbour and showed off our nice pink inside to anyone who wanted to view it although the Swain began exacting his revenge and spoiled our day by ordering the two screen doors from the cross passage to the upper deck to be kept closed whilst alongside. Yorky and Mad Jock did, however, re-balance the books a little one evening by smuggling aboard, under his very eyes, a frightful looking female whom they entertained down in the bosun's store. She left the ship after midnight with a broad grin on her face.

After leaving Poole, we loped up to the Needles on a long easterly swell, the ship's yawing motion ruining any chance we may have had of watching *Match of the Day* through the snowstorm. Once inside the Solent, we went to harbour stations: 'Special Sea Dutymen, close all water tight doors and hatches'. Rounding the Nab tower, we made for the entrance to Portsmouth Dockyard. When entering Portsmouth harbour, to port and just inside the breakwater lay HMS *Dolphin*, the submarine base. A little further on and to starboard, is Flagstaff Steps, the nerve centre of the Flag Officer Portsmouth. From this control tower, all ships leaving or entering the harbour pass under his and his staff's critical gaze. Ships are scrutinised minutely for anything at all that may be out of place or unseamanlike. If fault is found, the commanding officer of the ship concerned gets to hear about it almost before his ship draws abreast of the tower. Our ship was no exception. All commanding officers and their crews make a supreme effort to put on a smart display when entering or leaving harbour, call it professional pride if you like. To receive the signal that something is amiss is keenly felt by everyone aboard, not just the Captain and his officers. We sailed serenely passed Flagstaff Steps, as we had done on so many other occasions, with all of those who could be spared standing smartly to attention at the guardrails.

Just before coming abreast of the tower, its signal lamp burst into to life. Rat-a-tat-tat-rat-a-tat-tat, it went, whilst our bunting-tosser took down the incoming message. It did not look good. Those amongst us who could see the bridge, watched the faces of the Captain and the Jimmy. They were expressionless. The message read:

> 'Someone under your command has a rare eye for colour. It is, however, wholly unbecoming of you to parade it before me in this manner. Please lunch with me tomorrow at twelve thirty.'

We were informed later that it was about as big a bollocking as they come. Why? Well... someone had inexplicably left wide open and hooked back, the starboard screen door to the upper deck. That was a major transgression in itself, as the ship was supposed to be in *Damage Control State Two*, closed up for entering harbour. The Tart's Window Box, displayed amidst the background of ship's grey as it passed beneath the eyes of the Admiral, just rubbed salt to an already open wound. For the Captain to be invited to lunch was not seen by him as rare bonhomie on the part of the Admiral and, I am sure our CO went there with grave misgivings. Ginger was later severely reprimanded and lost a Good Conduct Badge for not ensuring that the pink door was properly shut and clipped.

On arrival at our berth on the old coaling jetty, just ahead of *Plover*, Scouse finally packed his kitbag and departed the ship and the Royal Navy, his time expired, twenty-seven years, man and boy. He was off, he said, to earn up to twenty quid a week in Civvy Street, whilst we thought we were doing well on twelve. We were envious. That evening we all went ashore to see him off. He was going to Royal Naval Barracks for a few weeks, in order to undertake re-training for Civvy Street and then to effect his discharge. Try as we might, we could not get him pissed.

He would be sadly missed, as he was one of those rare guys who was able to command respect and obedience amongst us with the lightest of touches. He always led by example. Whatever we did in that ship, Scouse was always first there, getting his hands dirty, his quiet authority and vast experience brooking any thought of complaint or disagreement from the rest of us. Scouse had joined at the outbreak of war and had seen action in HMS *Repulse* in the Far East. His relief, Leading Seaman 'Jumper' Collins, joined the ship a few days after Scouse had taken his leave of us. Jumper was a much younger man and had a totally different way about him. He was not so easy to get close to and did not have the life experiences of his predecessor. He was, however, extremely efficient and able and, in time, became well-liked by the rest of us.

8.   A Smokescreen Over Cowes

From 'Ratlin Down'

Now the captains sextant's brought us
To the place the chart has taught us
That the weather will be balmy
And the sun is here to stay
Now we have less cause to worry
Now that life is not a hurry
We'll be redding up tomorrow
But we're ratlin down today

N art Bruen/R Barr

We took summer leave early, owing to our forthcoming visit to Cowes. Once again, I managed to take retard leave. Whilst the main leave party was away, the Jimmy partially changed his mind and had us repaint the cross passageways and the insides of the screen doors "...so as to reduce the impact of a repeat performance when passing Flagstaff Steps next time."

We few who were left, thought it was 'get your own back time', so we took the paintwork back to basic white. During that short period, I, being the only one left aboard with any experience of cooking, returned to the galley, where, fortunately for me and the remainder of those aboard, there were no repeats of previous calamities. The moose nightmare was long since confined to history. When Dolly was on leave, the Swain stayed on board, so there was always one of the two available to proceed ashore and procure our rations.

One insignificant morning during that leave period, I was busy peeling potatoes next to the short brow leading ashore. I was seated on a chair, where I had a large fanny of water on a smaller stool between my legs. The Swain was just about to step ashore to collect the daily victuals when I stood up to make room for him to pass. In doing so, I accidentally upset the fanny of water containing a couple of dozen or so peeled potatoes. The fanny hit him just below the knee, drenching his trouser legs, nothing more. He immediately turned upon me, declaring, 'Barr, you are the most unable seaman I've ever had the misfortune to know!" before shaking his leg like a dog and proceeding on his way. I was about to remonstrate that it was not 'proper' able seaman's work that I was engaged in, but thought better of it. Leave was just around the corner and I did not want that jeopardised in any way whatsoever.

Having no car now, I turned my attentions to arranging my travel home when my turn came to take leave. To get to Birmingham, one had a choice between coach and rail. The Southdown Bus company laid on coaches from Portsmouth to all the major cities on a Friday afternoon, returning overnight on Sunday. Their green coaches were lined up outside Aggie Weston's in Queen Street, their destinations promulgated in large letters in their windscreens:– Glasgow, Liverpool, Plymouth, Sheffield, Birmingham, Leeds and so forth. Multitudes of sailors would descend to them from the dockyard and surrounding shore establishments, most with just moments to spare before departure at four thirty. Hundreds of others would scamper to either Portsmouth Harbour or Portsmouth and Southsea railway stations to catch trains.

The coach journey time to Birmingham Bull Ring was five hours, or thereabouts. It was not much shorter by rail. The latter, however, necessitated travelling via London Waterloo and then crossing by tube or taxi to either Euston or Paddington for connections. The coach was cramped and slow but the cross-London journey was tiresome and often frustrating, both outgoing on a Friday evening and returning during the early hours of Monday morning. You took your choice. As I now no longer owned a car and had just one rail warrant left, I quite naturally chose to travel by British Rail. At least on this occasion I would not have to face the formal ritual of falling in for inspection prior to proceeding ashore. On board *Rampart* one simply presented oneself in front of either the Swain or the Officer of the Day at the appointed time and asked 'permission please, to proceed ashore.' In Barracks and on larger ships, liberty men going on night, weekend or annual leave were piped to "Fall in for inspection", a time consuming exercise, particularly if you had a coach or train to catch. This is an example of the routine in Royal Naval Barracks on a typical Friday afternoon.

First the pipe "Clear up decks, liberty men to clean" was made at 3:45. This was the signal for the mad rush to messes, bathrooms, No.1 suits, *phoo-phoo powder* [talc] and bottles of cologne. Half an hour later "Liberty men muster at the Main Gate" was piped. This was the signal for the second mad rush – from the messes and bathrooms to the main gate. Woe betide anyone found skulking around or near the gate prior to that pipe. It was just inside the Main Gate that those of us proceeding ashore were fallen into three ranks, inspected and reminded that 'Liberty is a privilege, not a right' and that the privilege may be withdrawn if liberty men did not arrive back on board at the prescribed time on Monday morning.

"Come on for Christ's sake, we've got bloody trains to catch you doddery old sod!" we muttered under our breath as the duty Regulating Petty Officer [RPO] spun out his address, reading parrot-fashion from his clipboard.

"You are reminded that you are permitted to land no more than twenty five duty-free cigarettes per day for each day of your leave..." he droned on.

"For fuck's sake get on with it before we all die of superannuation," muttered the guy next to me.

"Silence there! Or you will be held back for a further fifteen minutes," shouted the RPO, looking up from his board.

This was the signal for the wiser among us to restrain the inclinations of the more rash from venting their feelings towards the RPO. Finally, the inspection commenced. A libertyman picked-up over his dress during the inspection was likely to be sent away to rectify the matter and, in the process of doing so, would doubtless miss the coach or train he had planned on catching. There might be other trains but there were no other coaches. That fate befell several people each Friday.

With the official address and inspection over, bags were searched at random and when all was deemed correct, the Officer of the Day gave the nod and the duty RPO would order, "Libertymen... turn right, dismiss."

There followed a stampede out of the gate and along the road towards the stations and coaches. This was also in the days before sailors were allowed ashore in civilian clothes. The relaxation of that rule, I think, came a year or so later but the routine remained the same, even when shirts, collars and ties replaced naval uniform for stepping ashore in. Until that time, if you wanted to travel in civvies and you were fortunate enough to have room to keep a set in your locker, you had to change ashore in Aggie Weston's, in public toilets or on the train. I personally never felt it was worth the effort and, in any event, travelling in uniform did have its advantages. In Birmingham, for example, I was never allowed to pay a bus fare when travelling in uniform. In those days, I used to get off the train at New Street, throw my bag over my shoulder and swagger along to the bus with a roll large enough to capsize the Queen Mary. Well, you're only young once! Then, when on the bus, the conductor invariably ignored my outstretched offerings. Certainly, in London no sailor in uniform ever had to pay for travelling on the Tube.

Paradoxically, Birmingham was fiercely proud of its sailors, although almost as far from the sea as it is possible to get in England. On one occasion, when in uniform in that city, a sailor from HMS *Blake* was picked-up by the police, taken to the station and charged with being 'improperly dressed'. On asking what on earth they meant, he was informed that he was not wearing the proper white lanyard around his silk. He explained that, as Quartermaster of the Gangway, he was entitled to replace it with a Bosun's Call on the end of a silver chain, but they did not believe him. Eventually, the local Recruiting

Officer was called in and confirmed that he was correct. He was released with many apologies on behalf of the Police force and their assurance that they always liked to see 'their sailors' properly dressed. It was only then that I realised how immensely proud was the City of its contribution to the Royal Navy, both in wartime and in peace; quite a sobering thought.

On this occasion, first leave party returned to the usual chorus of mild abuse and the next day we, the retard party, took our leave. Thankfully, this time, the journey home was quite forgettable. One Saturday afternoon during that leave I took my father to St Andrews football stadium, where we stood transfixed at the Railway End, suffering the accustomed deflation as the Blues, once again, struggled manfully to wrest defeat from certain victory against the Villa. Upon leaving the stadium after the final whistle, we were jostled and pushed as was usual when passing through the narrow exit gates. My father, feeling a less than subtle shove from the side, suddenly put his hand up to check the inside pocket of his jacket and found, to his dismay, that his wallet had been spirited away. There was nothing we could do in that constricted melee but I did feel so sorry for him. There was precious little money in it, because he never had that much, but gone was the lovely little photo he kept of my brother, who had died of pneumonia, aged five, the only photo like it that he had of him. My father never went to a match there again and was inconsolable for weeks afterwards.

If my homeward journey was unworthy of mention, the return journey to Portsmouth is definitely worth recounting. My midnight train from Birmingham arrived in Euston at 4:25am on Monday morning. The last connection to Portsmouth capable of getting me back aboard in time, failing which I would be declared 'Absent Without Leave', departed Waterloo at five past five. Whenever returning by rail, it was always a mad rush to find a taxi and to impress upon the driver the severe penalties you faced if, for any reason whatsoever, he could not deliver you to Waterloo in time to catch your connection. It was always frustrating because London taxi drivers do not like travelling light when there are possible fares to be had still piling out of an incoming train.

I grabbed the first cab driver I saw and bribed him with cash, saying, "Get me to Waterloo by five."

"Yeah, OK mate, hop in," he said.

I then spent a frustrating four or five minutes more whilst he arranged a further two fares that he could drop off on the way there. Looking out of the window as we sped off towards Waterloo, I watched the dawn breaking on another cheerless day, revealing drab, grey buildings and dreary, jaded streets that were still interspersed with bomb-site gaps left from the war. Just then, a strange foreboding overcame me. I could not quite explain it. We arrived at Waterloo with just minutes to spare and, after paying the taxi driver off, I ran for my life onto the curved concourse and down to Platform 21 – the platform from which the 5:05 train to Portsmouth Harbour departed. Without stopping, I flashed my ticket to no-one at the gate and ran for the train, which, was just beginning to move off. Opening the first door I came to, I pulled myself and my holdall inside and flopped down in a seat, exhausted. I had made it by the skin of my teeth. The carriage was a non corridor type, with only an exit door out onto the platform at either side. Better still, it was warm and it was empty. That meant a lie down and an hour and fifty minutes' sleep. Whoopee! I was surprised to find that there were not more passengers about, as normally this was a train crowded with Matelots returning from leave. But so what? More room for me and next stop Portsmouth. I stretched out and was soon lost in dreams.

I dreamed of all kinds of things but eventually of being imprisoned in the bowels of a ship swaying from side to side, of dankness, darkness and the cold. I woke with a start. It was nearly daylight. I was chilled to the marrow and everything around me was still and silent. The foreboding I had felt earlier came back to me. I sat bolt upright for a moment or two, then swung my legs down. 'Where am I? What time is it?' Glancing quickly through the window to either side, I could see only other carriages. They were just like the one I was in, empty and stationary. I went to the door nearest to me, pulled the strap and, dropping the window, stuck my head out. Looking up and down the track, I could see nothing except carriages. Crossing to the other side, I did the same. No different, but this time I thought I could make out station buildings in the distance ahead. My watch said six fifteen.

Shit, I was going to be late! Grabbing my grip, I opened the door and, without looking down, jumped to the track bed below, landing like a sack of spuds.

'Christ alive! That was a long drop,' I thought to myself as I stood up and brushed the dirt from my trouser legs, then 'God help me, I'm in a poxy siding!'

I turned and hobbled off in the direction of what I took to be a station. It was difficult terrain upon which to run, so I slowed to a fast walk. "Where the hell am I?" I said out loud to myself. "This is all I bloody need." Eventually, I reached the end of the row of carriages and saw two platform ends slightly off to my right. Gaining the nearest of them, I slowed to a more nonchalant walk, hoping not to raise suspicion as to where I had come from. I need not have worried. Those about at that time of the morning were too busy with their noses stuck into *The Times* or *The Telegraph* to pay any attention to a wandering Matelot. Looking up, I saw 'ALDERSHOT' written on the platform signboard.

"Bloody hell! Where's the ticket office?" I asked no one in particular. Not waiting for an answer, I ran on and found it myself. There, I had to purchase a ticket, my old one not being routed via Aldershot, and caught the next fast train to Portsmouth. I eventually arrived aboard *Rampart* at nine fifteen, an hour and a half adrift. At eleven, I was mustered in front of the Captain's table as a defaulter. For company, I had Jock and Yorky, who were there after being detained by the Naval Shore Patrol following a disturbance in the Lennox on the previous night. I was first up.

"Able Seaman Barr!" shouted the Swain.

"Sir!" I replied, stepping forward two paces.

"Off Caps!"

I responded smartly.

The Swain then read out the charge.

"Able Seaman Barr, Sir, did without permission, extend his leave and arrived on board one hour and thirty minutes adrift... Sir!"

The Captain looked at me resignedly.

"This is a very serious offence, Able Seaman Barr. Before I pronounce punishment, have you anything to say in mitigation?" he said gently.

"Well sir..." I began. "On arrival at Euston Station and whilst waiting for a taxi to Waterloo, I spotted a very frail, grey haired lady attempting to board a train opposite me. She was loaded with cases and was struggling to lift them into the carriage, there being no porters about to help her. Being in such a long queue and thinking that I had time to do her a good turn and still catch a taxi, I ran across and asked if I could help her. "Oh! Thank you." she replied gratefully, then, looking at me exclaimed, "My, my, you're a sailor. My late husband was the Captain of HMS *Swiftsure* you know, did you know him by the way? No? Well anyway, you are a credit to his memory, God Bless you young man," she said to me as I helped her on with the rest of her cases, Sir! I then ran back for a taxi. Unfortunately, by the time I got back into the queue, they had all gone and, when I did get one, it got me to Waterloo too late for me to catch my train to Portsmouth, Sir."

I could see, out of the corner of my eye, the Swain nearly choking himself with rage, but I kept going nonetheless.

"I would do exactly the same again in similar circumstances, Sir." I said, with greater boldness than I thought I possessed.

The Captain looked hard into my eyes for a moment before replying.

"The punishment for overstaying your leave entitlement, as well you know, Able Seaman Barr, is the withdrawal of that privilege. I do not condone absence without leave under any circumstances whatsoever. Neither, incidentally, do I believe a word of what you have just told me. However, on this occasion, and this occasion only, I have decided to reduce the punishment to five days stoppage of leave, since your excuse is the most original I have heard since joining this ship. Make sure that you never come before me again on a similar charge." He turned to the Swain. "Five days stoppage of leave, Coxswain."

"Five days stoppage of leave Sir," repeated the Swain. "On caps, left turn, quick march," he hissed, eyeing me contemptuously. "And wait for me outside my cabin," he added.

After dealing with Yorky and Jock he caught up with me at his cabin door.

"Don't you ever pull another stunt like that in this ship," he said, glaring at me. "Do you take me for an idiot or what, having the mendacity to come up with an excuse like that?"

I decided to say nothing.

"What is this man's Navy coming to?" He mumbled, as he went to his bureau to deposit the punishment book. "What have you got to say for yourself, eh?" He looked me full in the eyes.

"Er... what does 'mendacity' mean, Swain?" I asked, hesitantly.

With that, he gave me one of those withering looks of his and I thought he was about to throw the punishment book at me there and then. However, he restrained himself, he being the ship's policeman, after all. Finally, he ordered me to explain what really happened. Reluctantly, I related what had occurred, after which he said loftily, "Well! Today you have learned an important lesson, young man. That is a far more plausible story than the one you told the Captain back there. I may have been able to clear you of the charge completely if you had stuck with the truth. It's about time you took life a bit more seriously or you're just going to waste away your career like Halliday and McConachy there."

I handed him my station card and went back to my part of ship on the afterdeck. Jumper Collins, who had heard it all, was making a *Flemish Eye* from a rope's end.

"Look and learn," he said, without looking up.

I did and I learned. I learned not to be so flippant in my dealings with naval hierarchy in future and that, just maybe, there was something in what the Swain had said.

Cowes Week was then and remains one of the most important sailing regattas in the yachting calendar. Sailing takes place over several weeks from the end of July for all classes of sailing craft. We left Portsmouth one fine afternoon and made the short journey across the Solent, berthing to a floating pontoon a quarter of a mile or so up on the Eastern shore of the river Medina. With Cowes Week being a Royal Event, the Royal Yacht *Britannia* was in attendance. We were there, so we were given to understand, to provide logistical assistance to the guard ship, the cruiser HMS *Tiger*, she being anchored just ahead of *Britannia*, about half a mile offshore. Most of us aboard had very little to do with the sailing or supporting proceedings, so spent the majority of our time undertaking maintenance around the ship. The ship's motor boat, not the most pleasant of craft, was pretty busy throughout our stay, however, plying between ship and shore with liberty men and between ship and guard ship on other errands. We seamen manned the boat out of working hours whenever we were on duty. Very often, the duty watchman in *Rampart* was pretty well duty-everything-else as well.

The rush to get ashore and participate in the hospitality of Cowes lasted three nights only, after which every one of us was skint to the bone. We could not afford the scandalous prices charged in Cowes pubs, neither could we purchase on board our daily ration of two cans of *gnat's piss* [weak beer], this allowance only being permissible whilst at sea. It was a situation liable to create problems, which it did more quickly than anyone anticipated. To try to improve matters, the Swain borrowed a film projector and several films from HMS *Tiger*. One warm and sultry evening, we watched our first film on *Rampart*. By having the scuttles open but with deadlights hanging closed, the mess bulkhead made a passable screen for a 'big picture' experience but still allowed a certain amount of air circulation.

I remember that, in the middle of one exciting scene where the US Cavalry were chasing Indians at break-neck speed across the screen, one of the deadlights opened, the chef put his head in, looked around and then suddenly ducked back outside – and all in perfect size and timing of the film being shown.

The weather remained splendid and the racing was probably likewise, who knows? One beautiful day when I was 'duty-everything', the Swain called me to his cabin door and informed me that I was to have the ship's boat ready alongside at 5:30 sharp that evening, that I was to take the Captain out to the Guard Ship where he was to attend the official Regatta Reception, thereafter to lay-off a hundred yards or so until called back alongside to re-embark him.

Later that afternoon I changed into my No.3 blue serge uniform, went across to the pontoon and dropped down into the motor boat. Completing the pre start checks – is it still floating? Has it got any fuel? Is there too much water in the bilges? – I wound the starting handle several times, after which the engine coughed and spluttered into life in a plume of blue/black smoke.

Casting off, I steered it round to the port quarter of the ship and threw the painter up to the QM. The ship's motor boat was fairly ancient and had only a single-cylinder Stuart Turner diesel, situated in the centre. I remember hearing the stoker responsible for the engine's maintenance saying earlier that it was 'totally clapped out' and 'in need of a bloody good wrecking'. It was due to have an overhaul later in the year, during the dockyard maintenance period.

The Captain duly arrived at the short, steel-rung'd ladder and descended into the boat. The QM and I saluted him diligently as he took up a position on the thwart forward of the engine. Anywhere aft of it, as he well knew, irrefutably caused asphyxiation. That position was reserved for me, the duty coxswain. There was not a breath of wind anywhere and the water was as still as flat Guinness as I cast off. First, I headed downstream into the late afternoon sun, before cutting across towards the Guard ship, a half mile or so away. Once abreast of the mouth of the river, the Captain, not wishing to be late upon his arrival for the reception, ordered me to increase speed.

Now the old boat's engine coped fairly well with half speed but anything in excess of that and it was like a volcano erupting with blue/black fumes belching from the exhaust. I was not aware of just how much until moments later. Doing as I was bid, I slipped the throttle lever as far forward as it would go. There was no perceptible increase in speed but there was a huge increase in black exhaust fumes. There being little wind, the thick smoke drifted just above the surface of the water on our port side, just about keeping pace with us.

It was so embarrassing. The water all around us was full of yachts and small craft of every size and description, all out on the Solent, taking in the sights and soaking up the atmosphere of the occasion.

Onwards we ploughed, right through the middle of them like a Clyde Puffer, laying down an impenetrable smokescreen. The Captain remained undismayed, keeping his gaze steadily forward, his thoughts presumably focused upon his impending arrival. As we got closer to the guard ship, I could see other boats lying off her, some of which appeared to be very spruce and natty barges, manned by sailors like myself. Wanting to make a good impression for the sake of my Captain, I pulled back the throttle to half speed, so as to give myself time to consider my options on how best to go alongside the narrow floating pontoon onto which the guard ship's accommodation ladder fell. However, immediately I slowed down, the plume of black, sooty diesel fumes overtook us and blotted out the barges which lay to port of me, along with pretty much everything else. I think that my Captain was a little unsure about what to do next but I drove straight on for the pontoon, undismayed.

High on the quarterdeck of the guard ship ahead, I glimpsed the first signs of excitement at our arrival. I recognised, amongst others there, what I took to be the Officer of the Day. He was the one with the telescope tucked under his arm, doing a fair impression of an Irish Jig, dancing around, beckoning to his quartermaster and pointing in my direction. There followed lots of waving and gesticulating.

'What are they all waving at?' I thought to myself, the first seeds of disquiet swelling in me. I held on my course, hoping to pick up their voices over the noise of the engine, as their hand signals appeared to me to be very unseamanlike indeed and unlike any I had read about in the Seamanship Manual.

Closing on the pontoon, I throttled back the engine and brought the boat alongside into the space just vacated by another. Absolutely bloody perfect! *Nailed it on the button*, as they say. I leapt out of the boat onto the pontoon and with the boathook, I held her alongside for my Captain to disembark, chopping him off a smart salute in the process. So impressed was I at my dexterity, that I failed to see the deputation descending from the cruiser, via the accommodation ladder, to the pontoon. My Captain stepped out of the boat without a word, where, fleetingly, he was ignored by the Chief Petty Officer and the *Snotty* [Midshipman], who were making a beeline for me.

"Coxswain! Take your boat forward, secure it to the boom and report inboard immediately to the Second Officer of the Day!" shouted the Chief rapaciously.

He turned on his heel, saluted my Captain and led him to the accommodation ladder. I stepped back into the boat, shoved her off and motored up to the forward of the ship's two booms, jutting out at right angles from the ship's side. There, I secured the painter to the bottom of the Jacob's ladder, switched off the engine and, reflecting upon the first omens not appearing good, climbed up the rope ladder onto the boom and then inboard. I was met there by the Quartermaster and the Second Officer of the Day. I saluted smartly, saying, "Able Seaman Barr reporting as directed, Sir."

The Second Officer of the Day, a rather elderly Lieutenant, stepped forward so that his nose almost touched the rim of my hat and immediately launched into a furious onslaught over my blind ignorance, my total lack of understanding of the Rule of the Road, duties of a boat's coxswain, naval etiquette, signals and boats pennants, etc, etc. Indeed the list was so long that I quickly lost sight of the beginning and began instead, to sink into indifference. I remember clearly thinking to myself as he ranted on, 'the Chiefy in Birmingham said nothing to me about life getting as complicated as this in the seaman's branch!'

As I peered up his nose, I could see a huge 'grolly' just waiting to be hoiked out. Suddenly he seemed just like me, another human being, just doing his best. I felt so much better. He continued to tell me that I was extremely fortunate that I had no Good Conduct Badges or a *Hook* [Leading Rate's rank] to lose, because if I did have, lose them I most certainly would. I was told, in no uncertain terms, to get back into my boat, cast off and stay well out of his sight until I was hailed to come in to take my Captain off.

"Aye-aye sir!" I said, saluted smartly, spun around, grinned to myself and climbed back out onto the boom and down to the boat. I was aware of the pair of them looking down on me as the engine coughed into life, sending an enormous column of spent fumes upwards in their direction. I cast off and gave the engine full throttle, as if to accentuate my defiance, then headed away from the ship's side. When I had put sufficient distance between me and the ship, I cut the engine and drifted silently in the evening sunshine, wondering to myself why it was that, when faced with any issue, so many of my superiors felt it necessary to vent their spleen and shout abuse. Many years later, in civilian life, in my role as a management development consultant, I often used these personal experiences as examples of how NOT to humiliate and denigrate others who may be doing their best. Indeed, I was able to use many of my own Navy experiences when providing examples of how or how not to get the best out of people.

I estimated that I had at least another hour and a half to wait until I got the call to close on the guard ship again, so I made myself comfortable. It was so peaceful out there. Every conceivable kind of boat appeared to be out on the water. Those sailing boats that were about, their sails hanging limply, just drifted idly around, as I did. Speedboats growled across the mirrored surface of the water, cleaving white, effervescent furrows in their wake. Whole families, it would appear, were afloat in motor boats of one sort or another, cruising hither and thither, some of them picnicking in the late evening sunshine. Pleasure boats from Portsmouth and Southampton passed by, their passengers waving gaily at anything that moved. As one, seemingly full of females, came within fifty metres of where I lay and stopped in the water, I stood up in the boat, waved my arms wildly and shouted, "Give us a wave all those who got shagged last night!"

The result was magical. The whole boatload, it seemed. They had certainly fared a lot better than I or my shipmates.

After some time, I spotted one of the many naval launches that were doing much the same as I was, heading rapidly in my direction. As it closed on me, it came around my stern with a growl from its big twin engines. Its Coxswain, a Petty Officer, threw it into reverse and stopped dead in the water alongside me. 'Great boat handling that,' I thought to myself as I stood up to greet him.

"Get a good bollocking then, cocker?" he shouted to me, then, before I had time to reply, "Where are you from anyway?"

"Birmingham," I replied, proudly.

"No, you fucking dickhead, what's the name of your ship?"

"Oh right! Of course! It's *Rampart* and it's up the creek over there," I said, pointing in the direction of Cowes.

"What you did back there chum was suicidal, you know. Didn't you attend the briefing this morning?"

"Briefing? No, I never went to a briefing," I said, puzzled. "Nobody told me about any briefing."

"Well, you understand the significance of these discs then?" he continued, pointing to the one displayed prominently at the bow of his barge.

"Well yes, sort of..." I replied. "They determine the rank of the officer that the barge is conveying."

"Correct," he returned. "Well, there were four barges waiting to go alongside in order of seniority, three of them, like mine, with Admirals on board, when you decided it was *first come first served.*"

"But I couldn't see them clearly through the smoke," I said contritely, continuing, "It's the first time I have ever done this."

I immediately bit my lip, thinking, *'What a stupid immature thing to say. For Christ's sake Barr, grow up will you!'* Without another word, the barge with the Petty Officer in it suddenly leapt forward and was gone, back to its fold amongst its lofty soulmates. I cranked up the engine and crept very slowly towards them, so as not to create another smokescreen.

At long last, after all the others had been hailed, drawn alongside and embarked their high- ranking passengers, I got the call and slid alongside the pontoon again, amid some frosty looks from the quarterdeck above. The Captain stepped into the boat and took up his position on the forward thwart. I shoved the engine into gear, put the throttle to half speed only, and headed off back to Cowes without a backward glance. It had been a humiliating experience and, as we went along, I tried to think what I should say to the Captain but nothing seemed remotely appropriate. To his eternal good grace and clemency, I never heard another word about the matter, even when, three years later, we served together again aboard HMS *Victorious.* He must have felt equally humiliated by his peers but never afterwards did he say a word about it to me. It is possible that he had other, more important matters to contend with just then.

When I returned to the mess, having secured the boat for the night, those sat about appeared unusually subdued. Taking off my uniform jumper and collar I asked, "What's up? It's like a morgue in here tonight."

Billie looked over and said, "Jock and Yorky are in deep shit. They are both under guard down in the troops mess deck."

"Jesus! What have they done this time?" I asked.

"Caught red-handed nicking spirits from the wardroom wine cabinet," said someone.

I had not fully completed taking my gear off when there was a knock on the door. I, being the nearest, opened it and was confronted by the Swain.

"Don't get changed, Barr. You and Duff will take the first watch guarding the two accused. Pick your Naval Patrol armbands up from my cabin in five minutes." When Duffy and I presented ourselves at his cabin door he added, "You will not converse with the accused under any circumstances. If either needs to use the heads, one of you will accompany them and stay with them at all times. Do you understand?"

"Yes Swain," we chorused and departed.

"That could be fun," I whispered to Duffy. "I can see you standing over Mad Jock whilst he's sat on the crapper with his trolleys round his ankles. There is only just room for one in those cubicles."

Two others were detailed for the middle watch and a further two for the morning watch. Duffy and I relieved the Wardroom Steward and Ginger, who had been holding the fort for a couple of hours already. During my watch on guard, whilst reading a book, I looked down on the pair of them and mouthed, "Why the hell did you go and get caught, you stupid bleeders?" They were stretched out in two of the cots below the ladder.

"Ah fuck 'em all," said Mad Jock in response. "It's time we were off this crappy tub anyway."

I left it at that and went back to my book, hoping neither of them would be wanting the heads before midnight. Duffy and I were relieved at midnight and we then turned in. The following morning there was a flurry of activity as people came and went, including, I believe, the Naval Provost Marshal. We were all informed that lower deck would be cleared at eleven thirty the very next day. The Leading Electrical Mechanic 'Topsy' Turner and I were detailed to be Close Escort, with Topsy in charge. The prisoners' kit was packed by their messmates. At 11:30 sharp the next day, lower deck was duly cleared and the ship's company, minus the accused, their escort and the duty QM, were mustered in the tank deck.

One at a time the accused were escorted by Topsy from the troops mess deck to the tank deck. There, stood solemnly to attention, the whole ship's company bore witness to the charges read out and to the sentences passed.

Yorky Halliday was first.

"Twenty eight days detention, to be spent in the Royal Naval Detention Quarters Portsmouth," repeated the Swain, after the Captain had passed judgement.

Jock McConachy then took the place of Yorky, with me close at his side, while Yorky went off back to the troops mess deck in the company of Topsy. Mad Jock received the same punishment and then he too went aft to retrieve his kit. At 12:30 an HLD [dockyard launch] pulled alongside and the four of us, prisoners and guard, stepped aboard. Yorky and Jock went immediately below into the small passenger cabin, taking their kit with them, while Topsy and I stayed on deck, sat upon the cabin skylight. It was a nice day and there was a lot to see. We would be met at Flagstaff Steps by the Royal Naval Provost staff with their utilicon and there we would pass over our prisoners. On completion, we had instructions to return to the ship in the HLD.

We pulled out of the River Medina and into the Solent and, from where we were sat, had a terrific view of the afternoon's racing. As we sped across towards Portsmouth harbour, clouds of sail were descending upon us from eastward. There was hardly a gap to be seen between the multi coloured spinnakers billowing out in their van as they came on, with the wind astern. We were travelling too fast to be an impediment to their progress. It did nevertheless, make me stop and ponder for a moment. Here was a paradox. There they were, skipping along as free as the wind and the birds on the air, whilst here we were, escorting two prisoners to be incarcerated for nearly a month in detention. It made me think again of my own situation, and, to coin a phrase, how desperately close to the wind I sometimes sailed. Maybe I should start taking more responsibility for my own actions. It was easy to settle into the 'us and them' syndrome. Being 'one of the boys and a jolly jack tar' was fine for a while but could I go through my life just being one of the boys? You had to put up with the chaff from your messmates if you demonstrated to them, that you were in any way ambitious and wanted to get on. 'You're turning Pusser!' they would howl in derision. Perhaps though, it was time that I started to put my head above water and look towards wider horizons. After all, I had a minimum of nine years to serve and to date I had achieved bugger-all. As the Swain had said. 'Do you want to end up like the pair we had below?' I made a mental note to have a chat with him upon my return to the ship.

I was brought back to reality by Topsy remarking that he had better check on our charges. As we turned the corner around HMS *Dolphin*, he stuck his head through the companionway leading down into the cabin below. His head shot back almost immediately and he looked ashen-faced.

"They're bloody pissed!" he croaked.

"How the bloody hell can they be?" I responded, shuffling back to see for myself.

"I think you'll find that they are just asleep," I said, quite unconvincingly.

The pair of them were propped up against each other on the bench seat with their eyes closed.

"Then look on the floor. If I'm not mistaken, that is an empty gin bottle," hissed Topsy.

At this, we both leapt into the cabin and shook the pair of them awake. They were not exactly drunk but they reeked of alcohol. I picked up the evidence, leaned out and slung it over the side. Topsy commanded them to explain where they had got the alcohol from.

"Where do you think? From the wardroom wine cabinet while everyone was down in the tank deck," replied Yorky, proudly.

The bloody bare-faced cheek of it! They had revisited the site of their earlier crime and done it over again.

"Christ Alive! You shits, that leaves us two in a parlous state," I said, while musing over my decision of a few moments earlier to become a more responsible able rating in future.

With no *rate* [rank] to lose, detention like theirs now stared me starkly in the face. Topsy would be dis-rated for sure. I could see it all so clearly...

Just then, the launch began to slow down to make its approach to Flagstaff Steps. I peered through the cabin window but could see no sign of our reception party. I looked at my watch and discovered that we were half an hour early.

Then Mad Jock spoke. "Dinnae ye worry ye heads ye fairies. We'll give them nae trouble and we'll keep well out of breathing range. Come on oppo," he said to Yorky, "let's get this over and done with."

With that, the HLD nudged alongside. We manhandled the pair of them out of the cabin and up the steps to the quay. Topsy had a word with the civilian Coxswain of the HLD, who said he would keep an eye on their kit. Anticipating that we had no more than twenty minutes to spare before the 'Provost' party arrived to take our charges into custody, we marched the pair of them at a good lick around the roadways bordering the many administrative buildings that proliferated that part of the dockyard. We received a few inquisitive glances from passing Dockyard Mateys but, fortunately for us, nothing more challenging.

We returned to Flagstaff Steps with just minutes to spare. Our reception party of three *Crushers* [members of the Regulating Branch] arrived in their utilicon. Having exchanged pleasantries, as well as you were able to with Crushers, we escorted our charges as far as the utilicon before letting go of them. They winked at us as we threw their kit in behind them, then the door closed on them and they were spirited off into detention. Topsy and I returned to the ship, where we spent a few uneasy days, expecting the inevitable call to the Coxswain's

Office. Thankfully, the call never materialised. By a miracle of naval drafting coincidence, I was to be reunited with Yorky Halliday and Mad Jock McConachy six months later in another ship, where I invited them round for *sippers* each day for a week. By behaving the way that they had done following the gin episode, they had saved Topsy and me from our own appointments with fate.

At the close of the regatta, a few days later, we departed Cowes and returned to Portsmouth, the Swain showing extra vigilance in checking that all screen doors and scuttles were properly closed and secured. Somehow, the mess deck felt quite empty without our two miscreants but we would have to get used to it as they would not be coming back to us in the future. In the absence of Jock and Yorky, Ginger assumed the mantle of Top Cock among us seamen.

"Don't commit the crime if you can't do the time," he repeated, over and over again, until we were heartily sick of him. I never recalled either of them complaining when sentenced; it just wasn't their way.

9. Shooting the Balloon

From 'Ratlin' Down'

Now the dolphins play around us,
Now the fairer weather's found us,
Now we'll make our clipper ship
As handsome as we may.
Now we'll make the paintwork ready,
Now we're sailing homeward steady,
We're redding up tomorrow
But we're ratlin' down today.

    N Art Bruen/R Barr

During a long weekend leave at the end of August, I travelled home and made a proposal of marriage to my girlfriend Jackie, it being the first step I thought I should take in becoming a more responsible person. Much to my surprise, she accepted, so we arranged to get married the following April. We were both 20 years old and had known each other for just over three years. However, in all that time we calculated that we had spent less than 20 full days in each other's company. Jackie was an only child, born and bred in Birmingham, from where she had never really travelled far.

"She will have to move to wherever is nearest to my ship when we are married," I told her mother, quite confidently, one day.

"Well, young man, I think you will find that our Jack will want to stay here with us while you are away. She is not used to being away from home," she stated, defiantly.

I did not contest her statement but my relationship with her went rapidly downhill from then on. Unfortunately, it never really recovered but, to Jackie's eternal credit, she utterly defied her mother, who was a bit of a control freak.

Back aboard, on the first Saturday in September we embarked a full load of Civil Defence vehicles. There were 'Green Goddess' fire engines (the same ones that have been since used by the three services during Fire Service strikes), field ambulances, water tankers and mobile generators. These were craned into the tank deck and parked with hardly room for their drivers to squeeze in or out of them. The following day, Sunday, was as beautiful as one could wish for. Under a cloudless sky, the normally bustling dockyard was silent and tranquil as it basked in the bright summer sunshine. Hard shadows were thrown across the approach roads from the plethora of cranes, buildings and ships. Everything lay quiet and undisturbed.

The Civil Defence teams arrived alongside and trooped aboard. Some descended to the tank deck to make final checks to vehicles while the remainder dispersed themselves along the two walkways either side of it. News filtered aft that there were a few 'bits of tasty crumpet' amongst them too. We all craned our necks to get a glimpse but the only two that I saw reminded me of Irina and Tamara Press (Russian shot-putters). At around 8:30 we slipped our berth and nudged our way out of the harbour.

The exercise upon which we were embarked was designed to test the ability of Civil Defence teams to react to a civil disaster in which they would provide assistance to the three emergency services. It was to be assumed that Civil Defence Forces were prevented from getting through to the designated disaster area by road or rail, they having been too badly damaged, and that the only other option open to them was to land from the sea. We were to ferry them to the nearest safe landing site to the designated disaster area, put them ashore, then depart for a gunnery exercise somewhere to the southwest of the Isles of Wight. The amount of information we received prior to this exercise amazed us all. We received our briefing on the Friday before embarking the vehicles, although the only bit of it I still remember is that 'fraternising with the females aboard' was strictly forbidden. I never did find out the relevance of the gunnery shoot.

After leaving the harbour mouth, we stood off Southsea beach, about two miles distant, and ran on towards its eastern end, around the vicinity of Eastney. I was part of the kedge anchor party on the after deck. The plan was that when we turned and ran in closer to the beach, the large kedge anchor was to be slipped, so as to enable us to haul ourselves off again once the vehicles had been disembarked, the power of the ship's engines, combined with the pulling power of the winch being sufficient to re-float us when the time came to reverse away from the beach. This we had done on several occasions previously, in Studland Bay and in Barnstaple Bay. We were to beach about an hour before high tide and, with the disembarkation planned to take less than an hour, would be away again just as the tide began to ebb.

Being only a mile or so to seaward of Southsea, we could quite clearly see police and civil defence personnel on the shingle ahead. It being such sublime weather, the beach was packed with bathers. It seemed, from where we stood, that there was not a foot of space between them. We slowly turned shoreward and commenced our approach. On the beach ahead of us, there was a gap in the crowd about two hundred meters wide. The police had cleared and cordoned off the landing area.

It was the first time that any of us had beached the ship in front of such an audience. On most other occasions, there would be only a handful of observers present during such an exercise. As we moved ever closer to them, we could see hoards of holidaymakers crowding towards the barriers, either side of the cleared space. The Jimmy came aft and, at his given signal, the Leading Hand slipped the anchor. Away it went with a splash and a whir of the cable drum. Several minutes later, we grounded ever so gently onto the shingle beach. Everything was secured aft and, with an 'anchor watchman' left on the after deck, the remainder of us went forward, ready to be of assistance to the bow doors party (and to view the 'crumpet' ashore and aboard).

When we arrived on the foredeck, the doors were open and the ramp already lowered. The beach, at this point, shelved reasonably sharply, so there was not a great deal of water between the ramp and the water's edge. To bridge the gap, steel ramps about twice the width of the vehicles' wheels were laid and, beyond those, a steel cable net was laid and pegged deep into the beach at its furthermost end.

By this time, all of the vehicles aboard were fully manned. With a wave from the Beachmaster, the front one, a Green Goddess Fire Engine, gingerly made its way down the ship's ramp and onto the steel wheel ramps. It then made its way, a little drunkenly, onto the beach, where it immediately became bogged down, to great applause from the watching crowds. Several attempts at shoving and pushing by all and sundry was to no avail. The netting just pulled away from its pegs. There was a delay of about an hour before assistance arrived. When it did, it came in the shape of a tracked recovery vehicle from, we believed, the Royal Marines Barracks just up the road from the landing site. One by one, the cargo was driven out over the ramp and onto the beach, where each had to be towed up and over the top of the shingle hump. At last, the final vehicle disembarked, but it was apparent that the whole process had taken far longer than anticipated.

At a signal from the Jimmy, we of the kedge anchor party returned to the afterdeck to prepare for our withdrawal. When the moment came, the engines were put astern and the cable winch set in motion. There was, however, no movement, just violent shaking. The ramp having been raised, the rest of the crew on deck were ordered aft, where, on the command of the Jimmy, we commenced jumping up and down in unison, to assist the process of getting afloat. The bathers ashore thought this hilarious and started chanting "Up-Down, Up-Down..." in time with our efforts. Eventually, the engines stopped turning and the cable drum brake was applied. We were well-and-truly aground and no mistake. The Jimmy dashed off to the bridge for a conflab with the Captain. Eventually he returned and informed us that we had missed the tide and would make another attempt at nine thirty that evening. Until then, it being Sunday and, after clearing up decks, the hands could go below and leave would be granted to just two watches until six thirty that evening. The seamen duty watch were detailed to their posts, one on anchor watch and, owing to so many people being in the close proximity of the ship, four sentries to patrol the upper deck. The rest of us dived into the mess to change, amidst howls of protest from the duty watch.

"Tough Shit! You shouldn't have joined if you can't take it," came the disingenuous reply from the rest of us.

Some put on sports gear and took their swimming togs with them, intent on mixing with the female bathers ashore that had already been espied. The remainder of us put on half blues and sallied off the ramp in the direction of the nearest watering hole, with, by this time, only an hour or so left until closing time at two-thirty. In the short period of time we had had at our disposal, we each downed four or five pints and a similar number of pasties, before making our way back to the ship, intent on joining the bathing party, wherever they may be, for the remainder of the afternoon.

Coming over the brow of the beach, we were confronted by a scene that would have made one of those wonderful comic jigsaw puzzle pictures. The ship was swarming with day trippers. They seemed to be hanging off anything and everything. What a sight! We quickly scrambled back up the ramp and fought our way through the throng.

"Thank Christ you're back, fellas! Help us get this lot off the ship!" shouted a very harassed member of the duty watch.

We all split up and started to round people up. I personally told them that if they did not get ashore pronto, they would be going to sea for a long time. Slowly but surely, we manoeuvred them back down into the tank deck and from there, out through the bow doors and ashore. An hour or so later, the

Jimmy and the Swain arrived back on board. They had strolled along the beach as far as the Pleasure Park and, fortunately for the duty watch, had missed all the fun. In the mess afterwards, we got the gist of how so many people had come to be aboard. The four so-called sentries had been goofing at the holidaymakers from the ship's side, feeling hacked off that they had been left out of it, as it were. After checking that the Captain and the Navigator were nowhere to be seen, they invited several female bathers aboard, through the open bow doors.

Whilst they were showing their guests around and fixing themselves up with dates for the following evening, the rest of the crowd, probably thinking that the ship was open to visitors, followed suit and clambered aboard after them. By the time the four of them wised up to what was happening, well over a hundred trippers had invaded the ship. We had arrived back just as they had begun to attempt clearing them off. It was a close shave, with the Jimmy and the Swain returning shortly afterwards. Apparently, neither the Captain nor the Navigator, both whom were aboard at the time, had been any the wiser. Fortunately, the hordes had not penetrated as far as their cabins or the Wardroom Mess.

One consequence followed this episode, however. During Captain's rounds on the Saturday following the exercise, several items of ship's equipment were found to be missing. Among them were two fire hose nozzles, a lifebelt displaying the ship's name, the leading cook's whites and the mess tea urn. It's amazing what people will steal for souvenirs! We quickly went through our private belongings, checking to see if anything else was missing, but they were not. At least the living spaces had not been penetrated.

We spent the rest of the afternoon and early evening watching the snowstorm on the television. Special Sea Duty men were piped at eight forty five, by which time the day was drawing to a close and, with the exception of a few promenaders, the beach was empty. This time, it being high tide, we had no problem extricating ourselves from the beach. Soon after, we were heading for the eastern end of the Isle of Wight. We went back into sea watches and proceeded slowly down the Channel. It was announced at evening rounds, that the following day we were going to have some gunnery practice for the benefit of the 'then there is also, of course, the Gunnery Branch' ratings in the ship.

We reached the firing range, somewhere to the southeast of Portland, by nine the following morning. There was a buzz of excitement from the gunnery ratings in the ship, all four of us, and cries of derision from the rest, who felt that they had been denied a night's shore leave in order to accommodate the excesses of the gunnery branch. We, the lucky ones, mustered aft on the gun deck to hear what was about to happen, while one of the stokers was sent down to the engineering workshop to fetch a gas bottle. Able Seaman 'Plummy' Duff, the rating responsible for maintaining the ship's one and only gun, an ancient 20mm Oerlikon, set about stripping the covers off it whilst the other three of us looked on in anticipation. With the exception of Duff, who had only trained on a dummy Oerlikon gun at Whale Island, none of us had ever been near an Oerlikon gun before.

"We are going to have a shoot," announced the Jimmy, when we were all lined up present and correct in front of him.

"Oh, thank you Santa Claus, just what I wanted in my stocking," murmured Ginger out of the corner of his mouth.

"I want your fullest attention," continued the Jimmy. "I will release gas filled balloons away to starboard here. You will not open fire until I give the command. What will you not do?"

"We will not open fire until you give the command, Sir!" we all chorused.

At this point, Ginger pissed himself, literally.

The Jimmy went on to give safety instructions and to explain the parameters and arcs of fire permissible, before dismissing us to receive some instructions on the functions of the gun from its maintainer. After Plummy had described the workings of the gun and its capabilities, he looked at us and said, "Well, you tossers... anyone got any questions?"

"Yes! Where the fuck is the trigger again?" Ginger asked.

"How many rounds are in a short burst?" asked another.

I chipped in with "What's the command to open fire?" and "What shall I shoot at if I hit all the balloons?

Plummy stuck two fingers up in reply and told us all to piss off. Once all was explained, we had a dry run, each following an imaginary target. The gun mounting had stops on it, to prevent you from raking the bridge with fire; if you traversed the gun past one of the stops while pressing the trigger, it would not fire. If you were to place a clockface flat upon the deck with twelve o'clock facing forward to the bow, then your available arc of fire would be from two thirty, round through six o'clock, to nine thirty. I remember thinking that it would be as well not to let the enemy know of this, or he would surely never approach the ship from the direction that we could fire our gun at him. The stoker pumped up a couple of dozen balloons, approximately a metre in diameter, and secured them to the bridge rail. The ship turned so that, when they were released, the balloons drifted off on the starboard beam. We were all to have five targets each and were to fire short bursts only – five or six rounds at a time.

Plummy volunteered to go first, so the rest of us fled the immediate area in panic as Plummy Duff had never seemed to us to be the most 'all up and together' sort of person to be in charge of a gun, particularly one with live ammunition in it. Away went the first two balloons, away and up, darting around in the wind.

At the given signal, "Fire when target acquired" Duff fired six short bursts *doofa-doofa-doofa-doofa-doofa* and didn't hit a thing.

Doofa-doofa-doofa again went the gun. Again no hits.

"Aha! Methinks it's not as easy as it looks," said Billie Addison, as he prepared to go next.

Doofa-doofa-doofa-doofa-doofa... We all peered at the diminutive balloons rapidly disappearing into the sky. Not even a graze.

By the time my turn came, second from last, not a balloon had been as much as kissed by any of the 20mm rounds fired at them. I was determined to be the first to score a hit, so took my time in trying to zero in on a fast disappearing balloon that was darting about like a bluebottle in a jam jar.

"Come on Barr, you wanker, before we all die of anticipation!" shouted Ginger to me as I rattled off sixteen or more rounds in the general direction of where I thought the targets might be.

Needless to say, I missed the lot of them.

Only Ginger himself, who was last to go, managed to score a hit. In fact, he scored two, a feat which the rest of us were never allowed to forget as long as I remained in the ship.

The shoot finally over, we commenced our return passage to Portsmouth, during which we received a debriefing over the day's shooting. It was accepted by the Jimmy that conditions were not ideal. "But when are they?" he concluded.

The balloons had looked huge when he held them in his fist prior to launch but once in the air they became tiny specs darting about all over the place. He, however, had been watching the tracer through powerful tripod mounted binoculars and reported to us that most of our shots had passed within an aircraft's distance of the balloons.

"It is not as bad as it looks. You would never be shooting at anything quite as small as the targets you shot at today," he said finally.

We should have asked him to explain this to our mess mates who, as one might expect, showered us with the usual derisive remarks when we got back to the mess for dinner.

"Couldn't hit a shytehawk at twenty paces, you tossers," or "Give us stokers a chance and we'd blow your balls clean off at half a mile."

For our part, we, the ratings of the 'then there is also, of course, the Gunnery Branch' remarked how nice it was to be among such valuable and supportive friends.

At 5:30 the television was switched on and we all settled down to watch *The Magic Roundabout*, a programme never missed by sailors in any ship on which I served. As we neared the Needles, we ran into a fog so dense that we posted lookouts on the foc's'le as well as the bridge. I was one of the foc's'le lookouts and, although I heard lots of ship's sirens and the bells on buoys, I did not see a thing. One siren we heard was so deep and resonant that it could only have belonged to one of the big Cunarders. It must have passed us by to starboard no more than a mile distant. At least that was the claim that came from the bridge when the radar plotter returned to the mess. Then, as if by magic, by the end of the middle watch, the fog had completely dispersed. When we arrived back at Portsmouth, waiting on the quay for us, were Jock and Yorky's reliefs. As they settled into the mess that evening, neither of them being gunnery ratings, they sat a little bemused as the claims and counter-claims of either side in the 'post balloon-shoot' debate grew ever more animated.

A week or so later, our Swain departed for pastures new, His shiny new Morris Minor 1000 was delivered to the ship and he received a great cheer as he left; more a derisive cheer than a feeling of real loss on our behalf. We all reckoned that he bought the car with the savings he made on victualling the ship. His relief was a much younger man and we waited in anticipation for him to nail his colours to the mast.

As the Jimmy had promised, the ship was to enter the dockyard for a period of planned maintenance a month from then. We were to be accommodated in Royal Naval Barracks for the duration and to travel down to the ship each day by *Pussers Blue* [bus]. In the intervening period, we were to prepare the ship for entering dockyard hands. That was the signal for locking or bolting down everything that moved to keep it out of Dockyard Mateys' reach.

Before de-storing the ship and packing all our kit, all the crockery, galley utensils, bedding and so forth, were packed into a *Chacon* [Chatham Container – the first ever modular storage system]. This done, the ship entered dry dock and we went off to Barracks, where we found ourselves accommodated in another large Victorian block. We shared a messdeck with the crew of a Blackwood Class Frigate and still only half filled it. After Rampart's cramped and cosy quarters this was as vast, cold and impersonal as I had found it to be when I had stayed there just a year or so before. Having to revert to 'big ship routine' again was also a huge impediment. We travelled to the ship each day for work and returned to our cavernous quarters each evening. Poor old *Rampart* was slowly beginning to lose its lustre. Some of our crew were sent on courses and we slowly began to lose contact with each other. Priorities changed and we were no longer the tightly knit community we had been.

The ship itself, for so long clean and shipshape, looked a real mess in dockyard hands. Parts of it were masked off by huge sheets of polythene, stuck up with Pusser's masking tape – that fabulous cure-all/mend-all/fix-all. Angle grinders spewed sparks in all directions and windy hammers rattled as paint and rust was removed in a dozen or more places. Even the evil motor boat was gone. Our mess, so long our home and refuge, was now home to Dockyard Mateys. They even complained to us about the size of our old black and white telly as they gathered in front of it each afternoon to watch the day's horse racing.

I must say, I was taken completely by surprise one day in early November when the Swain called me over to him and handed me a draft chit. It read, "Able Seaman Barr, For HMS *Bellerophon*, 16 December 1961." So the old routine was to start all over again – plunged into the unknown, joining a new ship and forging new friendships. I really didn't know whether to be pleased or sad. One thing I was absolutely sure about though; I would never be as fortunate again to serve in a ship like *Rampart*. Nor would I be likely to rekindle the close friendships and camaraderie that had been established within her.

My new draft was to the Reserve Fleet. All those sad ships lashed together that I had viewed from the painting nets of HMS *Albion* fourteen months previously. Two ships, the cruiser *Sheffield* and the accommodation ship *Mull of Galloway*, an ex-wartime liberty ship, constituted the hub of the Reserve Fleet. I could see them both from the deck of *Rampart* as the Swain gave me the news.

I asked him if I could request to undertake the professional course for Leading Seaman at the School of Seamanship. He gave me the affirmative, so my request was duly granted and passed to the drafting authority. It would also be from *Bellerophon* that I would be married and from where I would pass the examinations for Leading Seaman.

So, with a heavy heart, I said my farewells to those remaining in the ship. My year and a bit in *Rampart* was unforgettable for so many reasons but foremost among them was that it was in her that I learned to become responsible for my own actions and that to blame others for my shortcomings was guileless in the extreme.

Whenever I think back to my short time in *Rampart* and remember the ship herself, those with whom I served and the incidents which occurred, it is always with the greatest affection and amusement, for she was the epitome of that most elusive of creatures – a happy ship.

10. What Happened Next?

From *Ratlin' Down*

Now we've got the trades behind us,
Southern storms will never find us,
Rolling home to England.
Butting flying sheets of spray,
Studding sails are straining homeward,
Dolphin striker bearing foamward.
We'll be redding up tomorrow,
But we're ratlin' down today.

N art Bruen/R Barr

Upon joining HMS *Bellerophon* in December 1961, I was detailed off to be the 'Able Seaman in charge of the *gash* [ship's rubbish].' What an honour! Together with two ordinary seamen, we bagged the ship's gash for disposal into the *Gash Lighter* daily. This lighter came alongside twice a week to collect the gash created by the over 450 crewmembers of the two ships that constituted *Bellerophon* – HMS *Sheffield* and *Mull of Galoway*. Our afternoons were spent cleaning and painting the sides of the *Sheffield*, from deck to waterline. I was left pretty much to my own devices and I kept a clean ship, as you might say. It quickly came to the notice of the First Lieutenant that Able Seaman Barr could be relied upon to carry out his tasks with the absolute minimum supervision. It was in *Bellerophon* also that I was reunited with Yorky Halliday and Mad Jock McConachy who, having done their time, were waiting to be drafted to sea themselves.

One freezing morning in January, I was climbing back inboard from the Gash Lighter when I saw, through one of the ship's scuttles, a PTI in his cosy little cuddy. He was dressed in his tight white vest, smart blue trousers and was ironing the ship's football strip. It looked nice and warm inside there, and besides, he had a transistor radio blaring and a mug of hot tea on the locker beside him. Cupping my freezing hands and blowing some warmth into them to bring them back to life, I thought to myself, *That's what I should be doing.* I was always playing games when I got the chance to anyway. Cleaning myself up, I immediately set off to have a chat with the Chief PTI, Bill Holden. Upon telling him that I was interested in becoming a PTI, I asked, how I should go about it. He looked at me kindly and said, "Young man, you need to be a Leading Seaman or passed for Leading Seaman to start with – and I don't think that you are, are you?"

"No," I said, "but I really am very keen and I have already had my request for a Leading Seaman's course granted. I am just waiting to go to the Seamanship School now."

He promised me he would make further enquiries for me and to see him again when I had passed the course for Leading Seaman. Upon returning from a long weekend early in February, I was chuffed to bits to be called to the School of Seamanship, where I passed the professional course for Leading Seaman. Upon my return to *Bellerophon*, I presented myself in front of Bill Holden again and asked, "Well, I passed... where do I go from here Chief?"

Handing me a request form, he told me to complete it and get it signed by my Divisional Officer. This I did before lunch the same day.

"Heavens above, young Barr! Don't be so keen," he said when I brought it back to him.

Then, at the end of April, quite out of the blue, I received a draft chit to join HMS *Ausonia* – a submarine depot ship based at Malta – a married accompanied draft with a duration of two and a half years.

"No way," I said to myself and my messmates. "I am not even married yet." I wanted nothing to get in the way of my PTI's course. Those around me thought that I had lost my marbles, passing over the opportunity for spending two and a half years in sunny Malta.

Rushing up to see my Divisional Officer, I showed him my draft chit and asked him to try to intervene with the drafting authorities on my behalf. He did so and my draft to *Ausonia* was cancelled, to be replaced by another, instructing me to join Royal Naval Barracks on 6th June for the Royal Naval School of Physical Training (RNSPT) at Pitt Street in Portsmouth.

On the 21st April 1962, I married Jackie and she did accompany me to Portsmouth, against her mother's wishes, where we took a bed-sit in Southsea. A week later, she told me she thought she had made a mistake getting married. We both put it down to early jitters and got on with our relationship without more ado.

Come 6th of June, I remember clearly the elation I felt as I walked into the RNSPT on that first morning, alongside 24 other candidates, to be told by the Chief of the School, Sam Johnson, to keep it in mind at all times that the PT Branch did not want us, we wanted the PT Branch, and that we wanted it so badly as to be prepared to go through a massive pain barrier in order to be accepted into it. A month later, only ten of the original 24 of us remained. On 18th December that year, the ten of us gained our *Clubs* [branch badge].

I went on to serve three further seagoing commissions: one in the Far East in the aircraft carrier HMS *Victorious*, one in the frigate HMS *Eastbourne* and the other in the commando carrier HMS *Bulwark*. The remainder of my time I served in shore training establishments. Unfortunately, I was never in the right place at the right time to do what I wanted to do most, run for Portsmouth in the annual Field Gun Competition. I did, however, train the 1971 Royal Naval Club Swinging Display Team for the Royal Festival of Remembrance, held at the Royal Albert Hall.

Sadly, like so many others in the service, my marriage was not strong enough to survive the lengthy periods of separation that were commonplace in those days. During twelve years of marriage, I was to spend less than four and a half of them at home with my family. It was always difficult, having been away for lengthy periods, to immerse myself back into family life and to pick up the pieces again. Many of those things that I took for granted to be my responsibility had been taken over by my wife and friction was inevitable when I tried to take them back again. We did, however, produce two fine sons, Gregory and Gary. The eldest, Greg, was nearly a year old when I first saw him and it took him ages to accept me into his life. Today he lives happily in Helsinki but sadly suffers from an aggressive form of Multiple Sclerosis. Gary lives in New York, where he has forged a very successful career for himself in the corporate finance world. I like to think of them both as being small chips off the old block, Greg for his rebellious nature and Gary for his determination. Who knows, they may disagree. Upon our divorce in 1976, Jackie received custody of our sons, both of whom were educated at the Royal Hospital School, Holbrooke. They deserved better of me at the time and I felt a great loss in not having been around for them at some of the most critical times in their young lives. I still then had nine years' service to complete.

I remarried in 1978, to my present wife, Stevie. She has a son and two daughters of her own, all of whom I am extremely proud of, and so we extended our family to five. Sean is a Senior Engineering Projects Manager with GSK in Hatfield, Nicola is a child psychologist about to relocate to Sweden and Danielle is a successful mother of two, who lives and works with her husband in Portugal. It was extremely difficult for us to manage financially at first, as I allocated 90% of my salary to Jackie and the two boys. So, over the succeeding years, Stevie and I took on extra jobs in the evening in order to make ends meet. We arrived home at 5.30, changed and at six thirty would go off to a well-known Little Chef roadside restaurant near Havant, where I, based on my *Rampart* experience, bluffed my way into becoming the late shift cook.

Stevie became the late shift Supervisor and together we ran the evening shift. We would finish at midnight, then I would drop Stevie off at home to relieve the babysitter before going on to a toy factory in Cosham for a further four-hour night shift. I still had to be back at my job at HMS *Victory* by eight in the morning.

Eventually, losing the will to live, we dropped the night jobs and I spent a year and a half in Cabaret with a great and true friend of mine, Bernie Bruen, whom I met in HMS *Bulwark* and with whom we formed a 'Jug Band' sometimes known as *The Malawi International Airways String Quartet* and at other times *The Magnificent Byzantine Minaret Minuet Quintet*. Arguably, the highlight of the band's short career was to play outside the Café de Paris, Monte Carlo, on the evening of the Monaco Grand Prix 1975.

Years before, I had learned to play the guitar and, with Bernie on fiddle and sundry other instruments, we had great fun working the South Coast circuit. During that time, we played a supporting role to David Nixon, The Wurzles and The Ivy League. We only dropped out of the scene when Bernie was appointed to command of a mine hunter in Scotland.

These additions to our main employment allowed Stevie and I to survive those first two or three years together. Stevie went on to join the RAF and became a Pilot Officer about a year or so before I left the Navy. What a strange twist of events. Saluting my wife and calling her Ma'am was quite a novelty for a while. It got even better when I found out her mess bar number and was able to drink freely at her expense!

Finally, in May 1986, aged 45 and as a Warrant Officer, I was discharged from the Royal Navy and passed outwards through the gate of HMS *Raleigh*, where I was then serving, for the last time, twenty-eight and a half years after first entering it. *Not that bad*, I thought to myself, *for a 'Very Unable Seaman'.*

I had already prepared myself for civilian life by undertaking a 'Start your Own Business' course at Plymouth Polytechnic in the summer of 1983. Having been institutionalised for so long, the urge to do something for myself was so strong that I pleaded with Stevie to help me start up a business there and then, so that the transfer from service to civilian employment, when it came, would be seamless. I scoured the papers and found a business opportunity within a week. The following month we bought *Harvest Home Patisserie*, a very small patisserie unit based in Tavistock, in Devon, employing just two YTS trainees. The business supplied gateaux, lemon meringues, apple pies and suchlike to hotels and department stores. It was going rapidly downhill when we bought it, having only three customers left.

There, we worked our socks off and, nearly four years later, suffering almost total exhaustion, we sold it on. By then we had a staff of nine, over twenty committed customers and a handsome profit margin. Being bakers was never our intent. The very difficult but often amusing period for Stevie and I – between re-marrying and selling the patisserie – is the subject of my second book, *Deep Fried Steak*.

What I wanted from running a small business was the experience. *Harvest Home Patisserie* gave me that. Following the sale, I applied for and secured the job of Entertainment Manager, on commission only, at a small hotel on the North Cornish Coast. The purpose of the job was to introduce Medieval Banqueting into the hotel. I was to bring this about, and take a share of the profits. I was also to be the *Master of the Revels*. This subsequently came to fruition, so I hired minstrels, serving wenches and trained them for the job. It was not too difficult, as some we hired had previous experience. Unfortunately, the location of the hotel restricted the amount of banquets people were prepared to travel to and so, several months later, the idea was wound up. Stevie and I then decided to do it ourselves and to take Medieval Banqueting to the customers. She designed and made over two hundred medieval costumes for hire and together we took Medieval Banqueting all over the West Country.

In 1988 we bought a small villa in Spain for holidaying. Unfortunately it was not completed, owing to the developer filing for bankruptcy. The horror stories, we found, were true. We spent the next ten years battling to keep our half-built villa from being bulldozed and helping to get the whole *urbanisacion* of 300 houses completed for their long-suffering owners, a task which was achieved finally in 1999. Stevie and I met many good people from all parts of Europe during those uncertain times, some of whom are now very close friends. Through visiting one of them, in 2003, we bought a small one-bedroomed hunting lodge in the middle of a vast forest in Sweden.

Besides organising and running the banquets, I also pursued a second career as a Business Trainer and, later, as a Business and Management Development consultant. My speciality was People Development. My skills, together with my unabated sense of adventure, eventually took Stevie and I to Russia, Ukraine, Hungary and the Crimea.

Together with four colleagues, I landed in Moscow on the day of the Yeltsin Coup and had to be spirited away into the interior, as no one then knew which way the wind was to blow in Russia. Stevie heard no news of me until a week or more later. During the next ten years, I visited numerous Russian and Ukrainian factories, including armaments plants. I lectured with others and held training courses and seminars in Kharkiv, Kiev, Topse and Savastapol in the Crimea. I had a front-row seat at the Russian Black Sea Fleet Review of 1997, whilst still officially a Royal Naval Reservist.

Together, Stevie and I engineered a trade mission to Budapest, following a conversation I had had with a government official there, who told me pompously that the English were all hot air and never fulfilled their promises.

"I'll show you, you cheeky bugger!" I said, and a year later, without any help from government or local authorities, we took a trade mission to Budapest. It was so good that we caught the Hungarian official with whom I had spoken a year earlier, with his trousers down, as he totally failed to meet his obligations to me. We drove the truck containing all the exhibitors' equipment ourselves, so as to keep costs to a minimum. We made no financial gain from it and the exhibitors did less business than anticipated but they all had a great time and remarked that if Stevie and I ever went into the travel business, they would be the first in the queue for tickets.

Indeed, we made no financial gain from any of our excursions into Eastern Europe, we did it rather for the experience. Believe me, travelling for three days and nights, third class, on a train from Moscow to Azerbaijan is an experience, as is being beaten half to death with birch branches in a Russian sauna or, indeed, racing a train to its next stop in a beaten-up Lada driven by a member of the KGB, or flying Air Crimea to Simpherapol in a battered and smoky old Fokker Friendship. We made many friends on the way and still correspond with some of them in Ukraine. Our Eastern European experiences form the basis of my third book, *Vodka and Chai*.

In 2002, Stevie and I decided to move permanently to Spain, and to commute to work in the West Country. We kept this exacting routine up for two years and finally decided to retire to Spain in 2003. Tiring of being so close to the British Community, we sold our villa near Alicante and bought an old Cortijo in need of renovation, 4,800ft up in the mountains of the Sierra Segura.

Our hamlet, if you could call it that, has only seven all-year-round inhabitants. This number rises to 15 in the summer months. None of them, mercifully, understand a word of English. We are now well integrated into Spanish life and culture and are invited each year to participate in the *Matanza* [literally, 'slaughter time' but today comprised of sausage making and the preserving of meat] and fruit picking. This year also, I was invited to repair the inside of the communal bread oven [*horno*], the ceiling of which had begun to fall in. Stevie and I take informal Spanish lessons from our neighbours, all but one of whom are shepherds [*pastores*]. Our tiny hamlet is set in the centre of one of Europe's largest Natural Parks (218,000 hectares) and is protected by UNESCO.

At almost 1500m, Poyotello is one of the highest hamlets in the Sierra, a wild and beautiful place, free from noise pollution and has no passing traffic. Our water comes from a spring near the house and we are inundated with fresh eggs, fruit, nuts and vegetables from our very generous neighbours. We spend much of our time exploring the interior of the Sierra Segura, its history and wildlife. We get snowed up in winter time, when temperatures drop to minus twenty on occasions.

In addition, we visit our small house in Sweden each year and, as a result, two of our children have bought houses there themselves, one of whom is moving there permanently. With our children living far and wide, family reunions are increasingly difficult to organise these days, so thank the lord for electronic mail, even if we have to operate it with a dial up connection only. Our experiences in Spain over 22 years provide the basis for my fourth book, *The Journey to Poyotello*.

Now I'm afraid that I must get on. Pépé is calling me to help him find a way of stopping water coming through his *cocina* [kitchen] roof...

Hasta Luego

~ End ~

HMS *Rampart*

HMS *Rampart* (formerly L4037) was a Landing Craft Tank (LCT) Mk.8, one of 31 delivered to the Royal Navy, initially designed for service in the Far East in World War II. With a displacement of 657 tons at light load and up to 1,017 tons when loaded, these vessels were 231.2 feet (70.5 m) long overall, with a beam of 38 feet (12 m) and draught of 3.2 feet (0.98 m) forward and 5 feet (1.5 m) aft. Retaining the open tank deck of previous LCT designs, the Mark 8 was protected by a taller bow section, fitted with powered doors and ramp. The deck could hold up to four 50-ton tanks, eight 13-ton light tanks, thirteen 3-ton lorries or 300 tons of cargo.

The poop deck was lengthened, allowing for an enlarged engine room, with four 12-cylinder Davey Paxman 12TPM diesel engines attached to twin propeller shafts, providing a cruising speed of 8 knots, a maximum speed of 12.5 knots and a range of up to 4,000 nautical miles. The expanded poop deck allowed accommodation for up to 48 of the transported vehicles' crews and an enlarged superstructure. Compared to other vessels in the class, Rampart had a higher forecastle (which allowed larger tanks to board) and an elevated bridge to improve visibility. The aft lattice mast was also larger. The usual ship's complement was 25. For defence, the vessels were fitted with four single 20 mm Oerlikon guns. Rampart was one of nine RN LCTs t take part in the Suez Crisis in 1956. Transferred to the Army in 1965 and renamed HMAV Akyab, the vessel was still in use by the RASC in 1979. Her fate after that is unclear.